Living Prayer

Also by ROBERT BENSON

Between the Dreaming and the Coming True

Living Prayer

ROBERT BENSON

JEREMY P. TARCHER / PUTNAM

a member of

Penguin Putnam Inc.

New York

Most Tarcher/Putnam books are available at special quantity discounts for bulk purchases for sales promotions, premiums, fund-raising, and educational needs. Special books or book excerpts also can be created to fit specific needs. For details, write Putnam Special Markets, 375 Hudson Street, New York, NY 10014.

JEREMY P. TARCHER/PUTNAM
a member of Penguin Putnam Inc.
375 Hudson Street
New York, NY 10014
www.penguinputnam.com

Library of Congress Cataloging-in-Publication Data

Benson, R. (Robert), date.
    Living prayer / by Robert Benson.
        p.   cm.
    Includes bibliographical references.
    ISBN 0-87477-920-0 (alk. paper)
    1. Prayer—Christianity.   2. Spiritual life—Christianity.
3. Benson, R. (Robert).   I. Title.
    BV215.B425   1998   98-15290 CIP
    248.3'2—dc21

Printed in the United States of America
10   9   8   7   6   5   4   3   2   1
This book is printed on acid-free paper. ∞

Book design by Marysarah Quinn

This book is for Mr. Siler, for showing me to the Dance.

And it is for Mr. Job, for the little blue book.

*And it is for Mr. Curtis, for telling me
who could teach me the steps.*

*And as always, it is for the Friends of Silence & of the Poor,
wherever and whoever you may be.*

Contents

Author's Note

MUCH OF WHAT IS WRITTEN HERE has for its
backdrop the two years that I spent in the Academy
for Spiritual Formation, a nondenominational
program developed and principally guided by Mr.
Danny Morris, with the sort of significant and
spirited assist that one might expect from his friends
at The Upper Room in Nashville. For a brief period in
my life, I called The Upper Room home, and still do
in various and sundry ways.

Each Academy lasts for two years and gathers four
times each year for a week at a time. Each day of the
eight weeks they are together, the sixty or so people of
the Academy attend worship three times, absorb six
hours of lecture and guided personal reflection from
two adjunct faculty, and participate in two hours of
covenant group with the same small group with whom
they meet for the two years. Some thirty to forty
books are assigned for reading during the two years,

and two study and ministry projects must be developed and completed with the guidance of one of the Academy staff. An Academy is intense enough and costly enough in time and money and effort that I would go so far as to say it is not for the faint of heart.

To really enjoy it, if enjoy is the word, it helps to be one part monk, one part dogface recruit, one part student, and seven parts hungry to learn to pray. Other than that, I recommend it to everyone. But you should know that nothing in your life will ever be the same once you have attended one.

The Academy is ongoing, with two or three beginning or ending each year in various parts of the country. The Academy I attended was held at Sumatanga, a Methodist camp way out there somewhere in the woods south of the Tennessee line and north of the Birmingham city limits. I would be more accurate, but I got lost nearly every time I went.

Some of the best people I will ever know were there. If I were to start naming names, I should have to name them all. They already know who they are. I hope to God they know that I love them, and always will, and owe them everything.

Namasté to them. *Namasté*.

Living Prayer

The General Dance

Accept the prayers of Your people, and in Your mercy,
look with compassion on all who turn to You for help.
Grant that we may find You and be found by You,
and that we may bear witness to Your glory in the world.

— From THE PRAYERS OF THE PEOPLE

Transcendence is . . . a progression from that which is given,
to its essence, and thence to . . . Being itself.

— On TRANSCENDENCE

The fact remains that we are invited to forget ourselves on purpose,
cast our awful solemnity to the wind and join in the general Dance.

— THOMAS MERTON

I DID NOT MEAN FOR ALL of this to happen to me. Or any of it, for that matter. I am still astonished by it all, and still a little afraid of it, actually.

I only started out to put a little formal devotion into my life, a kind of crash course in organized prayer. At best, I had this vague notion of wanting to be a person whose first words in the morning were a prayer, a prayer that rose up in me as I rose up in bed. I am not even very certain where that notion came from. But since the day that it entered my head, nothing in my life is the same. Everything has changed—utterly, completely, irrevocably.

It started out harmlessly enough: My father had given me a copy of a book that he had been talking about for some months. There was a note inside: "Your brother and sister and Mom and I have been sort of going along through this book together. Next week we will be on week #17—Dad." Unbeknownst to him, I already had a copy of the book, he and I had been talking about it, and I confess that I did not even open the copy that he gave me until years later. The note was inside the front cover and I did not see it until he had been dead for two years. There were a lot of things to which I was not paying much attention in those days.

It is a small book, bound in blue leather, with a gold cross stamped on the front and three silk ribbons inside. Its pages are made of Bible paper. The book is divided into fifty-two weeks, laid out against the liturgical calendar, with a pattern to follow for prayer and scripture and reading and meditation each day and each week.

I cannot say exactly what motivated me to open the book on the particular March day that I finally did, how much of it was a deep sense of wanting to begin a disciplined routine of prayer and devotion, or how much of it had to do with marking my father's passing and wanting to be near him again in some way. It is clear now that I was being drawn slowly but steadily to a life that was more quiet, more contemplative, as I have come to know it to be called.

The morning I came across the book, I was working in a loft studio that my father helped me to carve out of the attic space above my living room. I sat at my writing table and looked over the rail and down into the living room at the patterns the morning sun was making on the floor below. I looked out the window through the fields of the farm across the way to see if the neighbors' horses were stirring yet. Beyond the farm I could see the steeple on a small church some friends of mine attend. I opened the book and something must have opened deep within me as well, though imperceptibly at first, even to myself. Certainly it was with no grand plan on my part.

"Painting cannot be taught," said Picasso once, "it can only be found." I think that in many ways that is true of prayer as well.

I do not write about prayer as one who knows the mysteries of prayer but as one, among many, who is drawn by the mystery of prayer. I never think of myself as a theologian or a teacher. On the days that I lead retreats, I think of myself only as the head cheerleader, and I am honored to be even that. On the very best of my other days, I consider myself a poet.

Sometimes I wish that I could sing or dance or paint or compose symphonies or build cathedrals to express somehow what all of this means to me. I wish I were a priest or a robin or a child or a sunset.

"I rage at my inability to express it all better," wrote Monet to a friend. "You'd have to use both hands and cover hundreds of canvases." A fountain pen and a blank page seem inadequate to me almost all of the time. Yet they are the tools that have chosen me.

Freelance copywriting and editing projects were what I did at the time to make a living. For me, it was the writer's equivalent of taking in laundry. My studio was pretty much covered up with piles of paper, mountains of stuff. I had been given a chance to ghostwrite a book, and I discovered that it was pretty hard to write a book in the same room where all the other work I was trying to do was calling out to me all the time about the deadlines to come and the money to collect.

Frederick Buechner tells of how he wrote for years in a Sunday school classroom at a church near where his little girl went to school. He would get up in the morning, put on a jacket and tie as though he were just like other fathers, and go off to work, dropping his daughter at school on his way. Then he would take morning prayers with the pastor of the church and go upstairs to write until it was time for him to pick up his daughter from school and head for home.

I looked across the field that morning and decided to give the pastor of the little church a call to see if they would let me work there. It was astounding to me but they said yes, I would be welcome to come and write there. It turned out that the pastor had known my father and he was kind to me because my father had been kind to him. It was not the first time that such a thing happened to me and I do not for a moment expect that it will be the last.

And so began a stretch of some months of rising early and doing the things that it took to help get young children to day care and preschool and so forth, and then over to the church to spend time in the sanctuary alone with the little blue book: reading from the saints and the scriptures, reciting the psalms, whispering the prayers, and scribbling in my journal. After a while, I would go upstairs to write until it was time to go and pick up the children and head off home.

Somewhere in that spring an ancient rhythm began to resonate within me, calling me, drawing me, compelling me to join in the general Dance.

I seemed then, and still seem, to have no control

over my heart's response to that rhythm. Like the way one's feet start tapping when someone plays a country tune, one simply cannot stop even if one tries. My advice is that if you do not want to tap your feet, stay away from the jukebox. If you do not want to pray, then do not go near prayer books. Once your heart has heard the music, it is happy only when it is dancing.

After a few weeks, they gave me my own key to the church so that I could pretty much come and go as I pleased. The church staff was small, most of it part-time; we never really knew when others were coming or going, and we startled each other a lot in the darkness and silence of that little church. Someone was always coming upon me sitting in the shadows of the sanctuary with my books spread all around me, and letting out a gasp that made me jump and reduced us both to nervous laughter and shy smiles and muttered greetings.

But sitting there in that place in that quiet, about four rows back from the front, and over to the left where a window let the morning light in so that I could see what I was reading, I slowly began to be changed by the steps in the Ancient Dance. I began to learn to be comfortable with the silence itself, and to come to see it as a presence rather than an absence. I began to learn to let my mind wander aimlessly until it came to rest, and later to detach myself from the places where it had wandered so that it might rest in the Presence. I began to learn to pray with a pen in my hand, scribbling in a journal the scraps and fragments of prayer and remembrance and story and recollection that came to me. I began to read the psalms in a regular pattern that brought them around again and again, until they began to reveal their mysterious power to become the prayer of my heart on the days when I would not have been able to find my own words to describe or express the joy or wonder or despair or fear that was inside of me.

I began to read from the saints and the pilgrims who had traveled this way before me, to pick up the bits and pieces of wisdom that were printed in the little blue book, to take their words to heart as sustenance for the journey. I began at last to try to pray for someone other than myself, making lists of names and muttering them up into the darkness, though I was not sure what those people needed or wanted or even where they were most days.

It was for me a kind of correspondence course in the school of prayer, Saint Benedict might say. And it began to change me in ways that I did not even notice at the time, and still cannot completely explain. But there is no doubt that I was being drawn deeper and deeper into something larger and larger.

It is a life lived at attention that I seek, a life in which prayer has woven itself into the very fabric of my days, a life in which prayer has become a constant, as regular as breathing out and breathing in. I do not know for certain that such a thing can ever be true of me. The witness of the saints is that there is at least that possibility, no matter how remote it seems day in and day out.

What I propose to do in these pages is to look as carefully as I can at my own experiences of the ancient traditions of prayer that the Church offers: the liturgy, the calendar, and the habits and practices of disciplined contemplative prayer handed down to us from the monastic tradition. I keep finding myself stumbling across the ways that prayer in the ancient way intersects with the needs of our own lives here, our needs for silence and stillness, for order and oblation, for community and coherence, and for the God Within and the God Without. Such prayer can be as relevant and powerful for us in our day as it was in the lives and days of the ancient fathers and mothers. I am convinced that such prayer has much to teach us about our personal and private communication with God and also about our collective and public worship of God. I am just as convinced that the words of the prayers, words that have been said for centuries by the faithful, have power themselves.

I do not for a minute believe that in these pages I can teach you how to pray, but I can tell you what has happened to me and what happens now whenever I try to pray. I can tell you about the things that I have come to see as steps in the Ancient Dance danced for the Ancient of Days.

"To be a writer," says Ellen Douglas, "is to bear witness." I can at least do that—it is all and it is everything I can do.

The book that I was ghostwriting in those days was someone else's spiritual autobiography. Something about helping that person write the story of his journey began to tell me the story of my own.

Somewhere between the prayer downstairs and the storytelling upstairs, I began to see and hear things about myself that I had never seen and heard.

Ghostwriting is a funny thing. In order to write in someone else's voice, you have to get to know your own, lest you be unable to tell the one from the other. One day I heard a familiar voice tell me that it was time to begin to tell my own story. It turned out to be my own voice. And it turned out to be right.

To break up the writing stretches into manageable blocks each day, I would take little breaks—sometimes for coffee, sometimes for a walk, mostly for shooting hoops. The congregation at the little church had started out together in a huge metal multipurpose building, and then as the congregation grew, they had added on a sanctuary and offices and classrooms and such. The room that was once its only room had been converted into a gym, and the room where I was working had a window that looked down into it.

I played basketball all the way through school, and there are some old shooting and ball-handling drills that I did for an hour a day almost every day for ten or twelve years of my life. I can still do most of them, and when no one is looking, I like to run through a set or two, albeit a bit slower than I once did. I have pretty much resigned myself to not being drafted to play in the NBA, but I do have two years of college eligibility left and one never knows. Hoop dreams die pretty hard.

Bill Moyers once asked Huston Smith if he had ever had any experiences of the Transcendent. "Yes" was the reply. "There are some moments when everything seems to just fall into place and you know that for this moment things are just as they are supposed to be."

It happened to me one morning that spring. It has happened a time or two since, and it may have happened before and I simply did not recognize it. It may happen again, but to wish it so seems greedy and selfish somehow.

When I think about my transcendent moment now, it makes me giggle. I grabbed a rebound, took about four dribbles to the left, and nailed a three from the corner. As the ball went through the net, I turned and stuck my fist into the air toward the imaginary cheering crowd that was looking down at me from the room where I was actually supposed to be hard at work. I turned on my left foot and went out the side door into the bright sunshine ("Ladies and gentlemen, the King has left the building," intoned the voice of the imaginary announcer who made me laugh out loud at myself). I looked left into the window of the sanctuary where I had been sitting in the silence each morning for those weeks, hoping to begin to learn to pray. Then I looked back across the fields to the window of the studio that my father had helped me build.

Thomas Merton writes of the moment when he was ordained and realized that "I was brought here for this. For this I came into this world."

In that moment I knew as clearly as I had ever known what I was made for, and was certain that everything in my life had conspired to make it so, and that I had finally muddled my way into it, or at least into the beginning of it. I had a simple, clear vision of what my life might look like if I was willing to answer yes to the new question that had begun to rise up in me the way the prayer of God rises up in the heart of the psalmist and the one who will pray those psalms. What remained was to see if I could find a way to put it into practice in my life.

In the little blue book, on page 115, in the readings for week 17, where I would have started in with my father had I started in when he gave me the book and the note, there is this sentence written by Nikos Kazantzakis: "Only he who obeys a rhythm superior to his own is free."

More than a decade has now passed since I first read that sentence. I did not even highlight it then, the way I did so many sentences in the book. I was not seeking anything like that at the time and could not have had any idea what such a sentence might mean to me or anyone else.

Nothing in my life is the same now. I do not live in the same house or even with the same people. Most of the material possessions that I had then are long gone, not by some great and devout sacrifice on my part, but torn from my grasping hands by bankruptcy or divorce or other crisis. I fight a constant battle against depression, and I live a life that pretty much keeps me out of the mainstream most all of the time. I am not complaining, nor am I bragging. I am simply trying to make the point that since the day I said yes to the tune that called me to the Dance, nothing has ever been the same. That is not to say, as some would have you believe, that everything has gone along swimmingly after my grand experience of the Transcendent. Much of it, most of it, has been really hard.

But from this vantage point, I can look back across those days and see that the rhythm of the Dance had begun to call to me. It was so new to me then that I did not recognize it for what it was, and for what it is.

A life of prayer—or the spiritual life or the interior life, whatever term one uses for this journey that we have undertaken—is not completely linear, any more than one's intellectual or emotional life is linear. It is cyclical; it turns and turns and turns again, and carries us along with it.

It is that turning that caught my attention then. It is that turning, that Dance, if you will, and its rhythms and steps and habits and joys and sorrows that draws me now.

If we are to live lives that enable us to hear more clearly who we really are, then we will have to learn to move to a rhythm that is superior to the ones we have fashioned for ourselves, or the ones a consumer society has foisted upon us. We will have to discover the rhythms of prayer and life that can be found in the steps of the Ancient Dance of the Ancient of Days: the liturgy, the Eucharist, the calendar and the mass, the prayers of confession and intercession and recollection and contemplation, the habits of reading and retreat and working with our hands, the practices of hospitality and forgiveness and being with the poor.

Our lives must be shaped by the same rhythms that shaped the ancients, those who have gone before us. Only then will we be able to take up our places and join in the general Dance.

The Rhythm of the Mass

Grant that the words which we hear this day
with our outward ears may, through Your grace,
be so grafted inwardly in our hearts
that they may bring forth in us the fruit of good living.

—From THE PRAYER AFTER WORSHIP

The Church, therefore, earnestly desires that those
who have faith in Christ, when present at this mystery of faith,
should not be there as strangers or silent spectators. . . .

—On LITURGY

The liturgy is the work of the people.

—SAINT GREGORY

A FRIEND RECOMMENDED that I go see a man named Angus. If my friend knew then how much trouble I was in, and about to be in, she did not say. Looking back, it is hard to believe that I was fooling anyone much in those days. I believe I was the only one taken in. I was in a deep and downward cycle of depression, though I did not even know that I had the illness, and would not know it for some months.

When I went to see Angus, I am not sure what I expected to find. I had met him a few times and enjoyed talking with him about general sorts of things: books, basketball, the Carolina coast, writing. He had started writing a memoir that was turning into a novel, and he was always anxious to talk about the process and wonder of writing. And I was always happy to be treated as if I knew something about it.

Angus opened the door in the evening and welcomed me into his house and brought coffee for us into the sitting room. He settled his tall frame into a rocking chair and I sat down on the edge of a chair across from him. I started pouring out this litany of woes that I had been carrying, a litany of the stresses and strains of trying to cope with the life I was trying to live: finances and young children, uncertainty about work and a failing marriage, tensions in my business and family relationships. I told him that I had been praying my fool head off, of course, the way one does when panic sets in, and that God had not only not answered any of my prayers, I was reasonably certain that God did not even understand the questions yet.

Somewhere in the midst of my opening tirade, Angus quietly asked, "Do you know the rhythm of the mass?"

I looked at him perplexed, almost stunned. Here I was pouring out my heart and soul and he wanted to talk about the esoterica of worship. I ignored him and pressed on with my tale of woe.

Within the liturgical Church, the order of worship for a Sunday morning has pretty much been fixed for centuries. You can go almost anywhere in any city in the world on any Sunday and the pattern will be basically the same. There will be some differences in the way that choirs process and recess, in whether the hymns are formal or down-home, in whether the sermon is good or bad, but the basic pattern will be the same.

My grandfather used to take us to a little Lutheran church for services at midnight on Christmas Eve. I was always fascinated by the ritual and the dignity and the formality of it. It was as though there were some elaborate dance taking place, a dance I did not understand. Years later, when I was almost thirty and living in Chicago, I wandered into a big stone church on Michigan Avenue one Sunday morning and I recognized the dance. It was the same one I had seen by candlelight when I was young.

After years of worship in places where spontaneity and showmanship and charisma on the part of the worship leaders were among the key elements of the service, the steps in this Ancient Dance reached out and took hold of me. The propriety of it, the simple gestures and movements within it, the reverence and solemnity of it—all drew me to it somehow and eventually to the One for Whom it was offered.

I read a story once in the *Atlantic Monthly* in which a man talked about how important soft rock-and-roll music was to him as part of the worship service he attended. "I do not have a pipe organ at my house and neither do any of my friends. I do not listen to organ music at any other time in my life, why should I have to listen to it on Sunday?" he said.

Perhaps that is the very reason, I thought, remembering the days when I first watched those processionals in the aisles of that great stone building across the street from the great mall known as Water Tower Place. Perhaps when we are gathered to "ascribe to the LORD the honor due His Name," it is not a bad idea to use something other than the same music that we use to sell cars and make love to and entertain folks.

To see the liturgy done well is one of the most beautiful things on earth. And well it should be. Russell Montfort, the pastor of what many regarded at the time as the most "Catholic" church in the United Methodist Church, told me once that he believed that on Sunday morning we owed God "the absolute best show that we could put on. It is okay if we like it," he said, "but it is not for us anyway. It is for God." All too often, we see ourselves as the receivers rather than the givers when we worship. God does not come here to worship us, we come here to worship God.

·   ·   ·

As much as I love the liturgy, and as much as I like to
talk about it, Angus was not about to slow me down. I
was campaigning for the title of the most mistreated
man on earth and I was on a roll. I wanted to get all of
my questions into the air, and I wanted him to get on
with the task of answering them so that I could get on
with my life. I wanted answers, not questions, and I
wanted them tonight. If he was to be the appointed
guru, then I wanted him to get to it.

After another half hour or so, I took a breath and
went outside while he made more coffee. When we had
settled back into our chairs, he said again, "Do you
know the rhythm of the mass?"

In the years since, I have done a lot of reading and
studying and learning about the mass and its various
forms and practices. The variations in nomenclature
and practice are by and large a function of the habits
and traditions and histories of different groups and
denominations. But the four movements to the
Sunday worship, wherever it is practiced, are the same:
praise and adoration; confession of who God is and
who we are in relation to God; the sharing of the
Word in scripture and sermon and communion; and

being sent forth into the world to take our place as co-creators and co-proclaimers of the kingdom.

Episcopalians may kneel when Lutherans are standing; the communion bread may be fresh loaves baked by the church ladies or little round wafers bought from the local church supply house; Catholics may make the sign of the cross while Presbyterians almost never do. But the pattern of their worship has the same elements—praise, confess, receive the Word, go forth.

"Yes," I finally spluttered to Angus in exasperation. "I know the rhythm of the mass. So what does that have to do with me and my problems and the solutions that you are supposed to be giving me?"

If he was not going to let it go, and it was clear after three hours that he was not, I was going to get it out of the way so that he could press on to his guru work and I could press on to the shining and successful life that clearly was my due portion.

"Well, then," he said, "you know why we always have confession before we receive the Word."

He had me. I knew some of the steps, but I did not know the Dance.

. . .

In any interior life, there are times when we do not know how to proceed, when we are uncertain as to the choices we are to make, when we cannot choose between this thing or that. We need a word, the Word for us.

There are times when we simply cannot hear it. There are so many competing voices in our heads, so many possibilities, so many viewpoints. We can pray for guidance, pray for direction, pray for answers, pray for healing until we are blue in the face, and still no word comes.

"You cannot hear the Word right now," said Angus, "because there is no room in you for the Word right now. You must live in confession for a while, until you are empty enough to receive the Word. That is the rhythm of the mass."

Fortunately for me, I was still a Methodist at the time and not yet an Episcopalian. The Episcopalians say confession after the scripture and the sermon rather than before, the way the Methodists do, and they do a few other things differently besides that. I did not know enough to quibble about which things go first and so I managed not to go off on some tangent and thus miss the point.

The point was this: I could not hear the Word for

me yet, but I could at least begin to see the way to get clear enough and clean enough to hear it if it ever came.

It took me quite some time to begin to see what the rhythm of the mass was trying to say to me, but what I finally began to hear when I finally began to listen was a Word so new and so powerful that to call it anything less than profound is to do it an injustice. When you pray, I began to hear, begin by praising God for the gifts and graces that you have been given. And then confess who you are in relation to God—the good and the bad, what binds you closer to God and what separates you from God, what you can do and what you cannot do, what you love and what you fear. When you are empty enough, you may indeed begin to hear God's Word for you. Then you can go forth to become that Word in the world.

Writing about the ways to reach communion with God, Saint Teresa speaks of the purgative way, the illuminative way, and the unitive way—the way of emptying, the way of hearing, and the way of being taken into union with God.

My experience is that you can get a pretty good

crowd together to talk about the last two—who doesn't want to be illuminated by God and joined to God? But if you announce you are going to get together to discuss the first—the one about being emptied by God—you must take care not to overdo it on refreshments. Empty is not one of the things that many of us aspire to.

In general, we are not very excited about confession, and especially not excited at the prospect of its leading to emptiness. We do not want to admit our sins, our failures, our fears. We do not want to speak of our limitations and liabilities and mistakes. We tend to be perfectly willing to talk about the pain inflicted upon us, but we are less than enthusiastic when it comes to talking about the pain we have inflicted.

It took me almost three months of writing in my journal every day to make my confession. Not because I was such an exceptional sinner, although I had committed my fair share, but because I was a world-class pack rat.

In those months I confessed everything I had ever done, I think. Page after page after page of sin and failure and hurt and fear and anger. Page after page of what God had been to me and for me while I was being those awful things in return. Confession is not only about the stupid stuff we did yesterday, it is also about the magnificent stuff God did while we were yet sinners.

It was weeks before I could look anyone in the eye. Then one day, it seemed as though I was clean and empty, at least for a moment. I seemed finally to have worked my way along to confessing yesterday's sins rather than having to keep working my way through the archives.

And I began to hear a new Word for me. Or more likely it was the same Word that had been drowned out and garbled up for so long.

The longer we hold on to the old, says the wisdom of the Ancient Dance, the longer it holds on to us, and the longer it keeps us from hearing the Word that we so long to hear. It becomes a matter of not being able to hear God's voice because we are so full of our own. We cannot hear the Word because our own words are in the way.

We cannot be filled with God until we are not so full of ourselves. Our hearts and minds, wonderful as they are, are simply too small. We cannot give our hearts to God, or anyone else for that matter, as long as they are too heavy for us to lift.

Such a confession, says the Dance, is not something that happens once, of course. It is an ongoing process of being willing to present ourselves to God as we are, over and over again. This step in the Dance, faithfully and honestly and regularly observed, is what creates the space for the Word to be clearly and joyfully heard within us, and then without us as well.

"Tears hollow out places in the heart," wrote Gibran, "where joy can grow." To be emptied is to create a place that can then be filled. "They that sow in tears . . ." says the psalmist, and which of us has no tears to sow?

"Deliver us when we draw near to You, from coldness of heart, and wanderings of mind," go the words of the ancient prayer to be said before worship, "so that, with steadfast thoughts and kindled affections we may worship You in spirit and in truth. . . ." It is the Sabbath. We wait in silence for the processional to begin. Some of us wait on our knees, some of us with our eyes open, many of us with preoccupied minds and hearts, with the weight of the world and more on our shoulders, it seems.

The choir begins its slow turn around and down

the aisles, singing a hymn, carrying the cross, leading us into the courts of the LORD with praise. In some sanctuaries, incense rises and candles are lit and bells are rung. In some of them, the robes are long and the pipe organ plays. In others, you get folks in their Sunday best and a hot piano and a gospel choir.

"Open our hearts and minds we pray, that we may perfectly love You and worthily magnify Your holy Name." We rise to sing our praises, to offer our thanks, to declare our joy, to receive our greetings and blessings from those who lead us. Standing beside us are our hopes and fears and dreams and sorrows. We cannot lift our voices in praise without them. They too are who we are.

The room is filled with song, and so are our hearts, in spite of ourselves. To be in the house of the LORD on the LORD's own day is "right, and a good and joyful thing." We look around at the faces that share the song with us. We listen to the words of the psalms, the ancient prayer, as it is sung or said or chanted, and we listen, as Father Ed Farrell says, "for the prayer of God that rises in our hearts." The anthems and the hymns speak for us as we do our best to offer our praise to the One Who made us, the One in Whose Name we have gathered.

"We confess that we have sinned against You, in

thought, word, and deed, by what we have done, and by what we have left undone . . . some of our sin we know and some is known only to You. . . ." and there it is in front of us: Who we are and who God is. What we have brought to the Sabbath Dance and what God has brought in return. It is not now, nor will it ever be, a fair exchange. We bring our brokenness; some of it we can hardly bear to name, some of it we cannot name at all. God brings forgetfulness, so that it might never again be named. If we will let it go, then we will be empty, we will be clean, we will have room in our hearts for the Word.

"Open our hearts and minds by the power of the Spirit that we may hear with joy what You say to us today." The Story is read, the Good News is proclaimed to us captives and sinners, who now count ourselves among the empty, among those who would listen for the Word, the Word that we are to become for the glory of the One Who has spoken all words.

A servant of the Divine Mystery stands in the pulpit and does their best to try to say what is unsayable, to explain what is, of course, unexplainable. We listen with empty and hoping hearts to the words of a fellow pilgrim, hoping to hear a word that suggests the Word, hoping to learn to live our lives in the rhythm of the mass.

The Sacrifice

Here we offer and present ourselves to You, O LORD,
to be a reasonable and holy sacrifice;
humbly beseeching You that we may worthily receive
the most precious Body and Blood of Your Son Jesus Christ.

—From THE GREAT THANKSGIVING

The devotion which leads the faithful to visit the Blessed Sacrament
draws them into an ever deeper participation in the Paschal Mystery.

—On EUCHARISTIC DEVOTION

The prayer of the Eucharist is an invitation—
an invitation to follow, to believe, to serve, to suffer.

—NORMAN SHAWCHUCK

I REMEMBER MY DAUGHTER'S first communion. If we had been Catholic, I suppose, we would have pictures and her dress would be in a box in the attic. But we are not, and so I have to rely on my memory.

She was six years old. In the Methodist Church, if a kid is old enough to walk to the altar rail, and too old to go to the nursery anymore, a kid is old enough to take the Eucharist. Methodist children do have to wait until they are twelve for the real rite of passage into the fellowship, which is drinking coffee in the lobby at all Methodist gatherings formal and informal.

In the place where we were going to church at the time, all of the pastors made a point of saying your name as they handed you the bread and the cup as you knelt at the altar for the Eucharist. It was new to me, both the kneeling at the altar and having my name said, and I liked it.

"Robert: This is the Body of Christ, broken for you," they said as they pressed the bread into my palm. "Robert: This is the Blood of Christ, shed for you and for the remission of your sins," they said as they handed me the little cup.

The day that my daughter took communion for the first time, she was part of a class in the church that was formed to teach children all the bits and pieces of the habits and rituals of the sacrament, so that they would know what to do when their time came. They had spent several weeks' worth of Sunday school classes learning the prayers and practicing the movements. All of the children and their parents sat in the first couple of rows together that morning. It was a kind of coming-out party. There was an air of festivity and surprise to it all that is not always present at the Eucharist.

One little girl returned to her place carrying two of the cups with her. One was for her little brother and one was for Miss Peach, her doll, she explained to her mother in a loud whisper. "They both like juice." Another little girl collected about a dozen empty cups on her way along the altar rail back to her seat. I heard her tell an envious friend, "These are perfect for a tea party."

There was an anxious moment as a child dropped her little bit of bread into the crack between the altar cushion and the altar rail. She spent several minutes pretty much prostrate before God and nine hundred of God's finest while she located it and reclaimed it and popped it into her mouth anyway. The minister who was watching had a nervous smile and seemed to be trying to remember what the seminary had taught about such a moment. Her mother just continued to bow her head in prayer, but something about the way her shoulders were shaking made me think that she had seen this sort of thing from her daughter before.

I have what one might call a checkered religious past.

I have been a Nazarene and then a Methodist and now I am Episcopalian. I do not mean that I just attended these churches either; I have been a card-carrying member in each of them, swearing my allegiance to headquarters.

First it was to Kansas City, the home of the Nazarenes; then it was to New York by way of Nashville and wherever else headquarters is for Methodists; and now it is to Canterbury by way of New York City. I have a suspicion that I am moving to Rome a few hundred air miles and a few dozen liturgical rites at a time—although my annual pilgrimage to the Greek Festival at our city's one Greek Orthodox church suggests that my final destination may well be somewhere farther to the east. It is a long way from Kansas City to Constantinople, but I am young and I still have time and who knows where this journey may end. Truth be told, I never thought the journey would go this far.

In the Nazarene church where I was raised, communion was not offered very often, once or twice a year, as I recall. When it was, the bread and the cup were passed on trays through the pews like offering plates, until everyone was served, and then everyone ate and drank together. I was in a Nazarene church not too long ago, and it happened to be a day that the Eucharist was served. The way they practiced the ritual took me back to the sweet days and the fond memories of the first group of people that taught me the Story and showed me its ways.

In the Methodist church that I was in for several years, the Eucharist was given on the first Sunday of every month, and it was there that I learned to look forward to going to kneel before the table of the LORD. This new way for me taught me the consolation of having the Sacrament placed into your hands. I have to admit that I also loved the notion that even though I was pretty much the same old Robert, I was now somehow good enough to be invited to the table. It makes me think of the Christmas dinner when I finally moved from the card table in the kitchen to the big table where the patriarchs and matriarchs held court.

Now I am Episcopalian, and the Eucharist is offered every Sunday, and a few other times each week if you can get there. From time to time, on feast days, our congregation celebrates a Festal Eucharist and the choir processes all around the church, up one aisle and back down another, around and around us, chanting litanies and songs to mark the feast and to prepare our hearts and minds for the moment in the service when we make our way to the table. It is a powerful moment to me, this dancing with David before the LORD—though I always smile when I think of one of the members of the choir telling me that they refer to the grand processional as the Holy Figure Eight.

I have taken the Eucharist in other settings as well over the years. Three of us took it at a little wooden table in the middle of a field once a month for a year while we had a day apart together to pray and to recollect ourselves. At a retreat, I took it once standing in a circle of a hundred or so, as we passed the loaf and the cup from person to person around the circle. It was beautiful, and it took so long that we all missed lunch, but no one cared.

Once I took it sitting on the floor of my hospital room. It was served by a young minister who came to bring me sustenance for that part of my journey. And once I even took it in a room with twelve thousand people who were served in little cups with plastic tops, where everyone laughed out loud in spite of themselves at the sound of what seemed to be twelve thousand little coffee creamers being opened at the same time.

I watched my sister and brother-in-law and sister-in-law and my two best friends serve it to the people who came to witness and to bless our wedding. I saw it up close too, because the bride and I got to be ushers that day and we got to hug everyone as they came to the table.

Ed Farrell says that in a conversation with a Hindu once when he was in India, the man said to him, "I know Christians. They are the people who swallow God." It is true, that is one of the things that we claim. And it is one of the things that bind me to you and to all the rest of the faithful.

My daughter knelt at the altar rail beside me that day and laid her hands open one on top of the other the way she had been taught in her class, and then she held them out as the minister headed in our direction.

"Robert: The Body of Christ, broken for you. Robert: The Blood of Christ, shed for you."

Then they called my daughter's name, and as they pressed the bread into her hands, they said, "This is a gift for you from Jesus." Then came the cup: "This is so that you will remember that Jesus loves you."

They say nicer things to children at the table, I remember thinking to myself. Or maybe they thought that I was not yet ready for the truth of the prayer that is the prayer of the Eucharist.

No matter where I have taken the Eucharist, or what variations on the ritual I have seen and heard, there is one constant. It is the prayer that is called the Prayer of Consecration. "On the night in which He was handed over to suffering and death, He took the bread and He gave thanks for it and He broke it and gave it. . . ."

To take the Eucharist, say the ancients, is to enter into the fourfold pattern—taken, blessed, broken, shared—that not only forms the core of the great prayer but forms the core of the life of the Spirit itself. It is the prayer that is to be found at the center of any life of prayer. It is both the action on the stage and the backdrop itself. It is both the means to see and the sight to behold.

I have always enjoyed the part of the prayer that suggests to us that we are taken by God, that we are chosen. "You did not choose me, I chose you," we are told Jesus said to His friends once, and I claim it for myself as often as I feel I can get away with it. I remind myself of the hope of it when the darkness comes, and I celebrate the astonishment of it when the Light is all around me.

I am happy too to think about being blessed by God as well. The notion of God being so taken with me that I have been given gifts and graces and a place to belong that belongs only to me seems so fine and good. And I particularly enjoy the part about being shared. It seems perfectly fine to me that something of who I am can be valuable and useful and meaningful to God and to others in some way. To stand with Christ, and with "all the faithful of time past," as the prayer book calls those who have gone before, is fine with me. To be among those who have been taken and blessed and shared by and with and for God is good.

It is the broken part that I do not care for very much. It is the broken part, however, that makes everything else about the Eucharist worth making over. The lesson is that Jesus of Nazareth—the most chosen and most blessed and most shared one of us all—was the most broken of us all.

The prayer of the Eucharist is the prayer that reminds us that if we are to be the Body of Christ, then we are to suffer the fate of Christ—we are to be broken that we might be shared.

If the Christ is to be seen in this world now, then what happened to the Christ must happen to us. We who call ourselves His friends, who call ourselves His Body even, must have done to us what was done to the bread on the night that He gave it to His friends and told them what was to happen that God might be glorified. We too must be taken, blessed, broken, and shared. We must somehow stop offering ourselves *in* prayer and begin offering ourselves *as* prayer.

We often pray to be chosen, to be among that number when the saints go marching in. We regularly pray for God to bless us too, even though most of us already have been. Most of us have more than enough. Many of us have so much that if we are not embarrassed at what some of us have compared to what some others of us do not have, then we ought to be.

We pray to be shared too, to be taken up by God for some particular thing to do and be that can only be done by us in our own way and in our own place. It is a prayer that has already been answered in many ways, although it may be unclear to us at times just how to live it out in our lives.

But it is rare to hear anyone pray to be broken. We pretty much pray to be chosen and blessed and then press right on ahead to the part about being shared; that is where the glory would seem to be, and it is certainly what seems right for us chosen ones.

We are not even too terribly willing to look for the joy that might come from suffering, or even for the silver lining that might be behind a cloud. We are God's chosen after all, why should we have to suffer? Why should these things happen to those who have been so blessed and have so much to share? We should be multiplied, it seems to us, not broken.

"If this is how You treat Your friends," railed

Saint Teresa at God one day, with her fist in the air and her feet in the mud and her well-laid plans falling apart and her eyes looking skyward, "no wonder You have so few of them!" Preaching to the choir is one thing, God, picking on us is something else again.

Perhaps that is why whoever wrote the Letter to the Hebrews warned them, "It is a fearful thing to fall into the hands of the living God." It sounds as though he or she had the scars to prove it. The One Who Came certainly had some scars.

I am convinced that there is a connection in there somewhere as to how little, it often seems, we are truly shared. We are not meant to be taken, blessed, and multiplied. We are meant to be taken, blessed, and broken. "It is not the religious act that makes the Christian," wrote Bonhoeffer in his prison cell, "but participation in the sufferings of God in the secular life."

It is our brokenness, perhaps even our willingness to be broken, that holds the key to whatever it is we have to share.

Wayne and I first met at a weekend conference to which I had been invited so that I could conduct a workshop about some stuff that other people thought I must know something about.

Wayne sat in the third row and cheerfully disagreed with everything I said for two days. I already knew that I did not know nearly as much as the organizers had hoped, but I did not need Wayne to sit in the third row shaking his head and asking hard questions and advertising my ignorance to the others in the room who still thought I was an expert. He kept turning up in my workshop all weekend, even when there were plenty of other workshops to go to, including the one for which he came to the conference in the first place. It turned out that he came into mine to kill a little time the first morning, and he just never left.

He would show up at the table where I was having lunch, when there were plenty of other places to sit and plenty of other people to argue with. He would appear outside under the tree beside me when I was in between sessions trying to collect myself and get ready for the next class.

He showed up again a few months later, when the same group invited me back to lead a retreat. Then he turned up a few months after that, when I went back to lead another one for the same group, only this time he had talked himself into being on the staff. He was still arguing with me a fair amount, but by then we had some running jokes and shared memories and we generally carried on like old friends. We took several long walks together that weekend and told each other about our journeys. At the time, I was trying to make hard choices about giving up some dreams and taking the risks associated with pursuing some others. I was also wrestling with the beginnings of some things that would later take my life apart, and I was hundreds of miles from home, and he loved to ask hard questions and I needed a safe place to think out loud. It was kind of hard on my visiting-guru image to be pouring my heart out to him in between sessions where I was supposed to be the retreat master, but he had long been certain about how shaky my guru credentials were anyway. He was a good friend to me that weekend, which was what he had been trying to show me all along. We talked on the telephone a couple of times after that, but then everything in my life began to change and we lost touch.

About five years later, Wayne showed up again, or at least his voice did, on my telephone late one night, a pretty good trick, since my phone number is not listed anywhere. It was in that time of the night when the only calls you get are the ones that bring bad news, and it takes a minute to get your heart to stop pounding so loud that you cannot hear the person on the other end of the line.

Wayne was in a mess of his own by then. It is his story to tell and not mine, but suffice it to say that I was in tears for him by the time we hung up the phone. He was working hard to extricate himself from it all and to do the right things for himself and his family, but he was still pretty wounded and afraid at the time.

Wayne had a question to ask that he thought I might be able to answer. He told me that it was a question he had already asked a lot of people a lot closer to home who knew a lot more about what was going on in his life than I did. As only Wayne can, he even told me that he knew what my answer was going to be before he asked the question. Knowing Wayne, I was not surprised at this suggestion that what I had to say did not matter very much.

The truth is that what I had to say did *not* matter very much. Wayne did not call me because I had been blessed with some great wisdom. Wayne called me in the middle of the night when his life was coming apart because he knew that I had been broken too. It was the only credential that I had or needed as far as Wayne was concerned. It qualified me to share in a late-night phone call when he was being broken.

Frederick Buechner once said, "To be a writer, one must be a good steward of their pain." I think that is true as well for those who would pray. To be such a steward creates the possibility that others might be healed by your witness to such a thing, that others might see the mercies granted to you in your suffering as evidence of the compassion of God for those who are broken. This gift of our brokenness is often the only gift that we can give or receive with any real honesty and with any real hope and with any real power. We do not demonstrate our faith when we live in the light, we show our faith when we live in the dark.

To embrace one's brokenness, whatever it looks like, whatever has caused it, carries within it the possibility that one might come to embrace one's healing, and then that one might come to the next step: to embrace another and their brokenness and their possibility for being healed. To avoid one's brokenness is to turn one's back on the possibility that the Healer might be at work here, perhaps for you, perhaps for another. It is to turn one's back on another, one for whom you just might be the Christ, one for whom you might, even if just for a moment, become the Body and Blood.

"It is right, and a good and joyful thing, to give thanks to You," go the words of the Great Thanksgiving.

In any life of prayer, one will live through and pray through seasons of great certainty and conviction. Seasons when one is acutely aware of belonging to God, of being chosen and being marked for some particular time and some particular place and some particular work for the kingdom.

"You are the fountain of life, and the source of all goodness; You made all things and filled them with Your blessing," says the prayer. Including our own lives. And so there must be seasons of prayer that are filled with gratitude and thanksgiving for those blessings, for the gifts both great and small that one has been given.

"Deliver us from coming to this table for solace only and not for strength; for pardon only and not for renewal." There must also be seasons of prayer in which you must pray for suffering, for brokenness, for the most blessed of the gifts that make us the Body of

Christ, and that make that Body available to be shared with any and all of us. "Happy are they who suffer," Jesus said to those on the hillside, "rejoice and be glad when it happens to you." You cannot be multiplied enough to be shared. You can only be broken enough to be shared.

"Send us now into the world in peace and grant us strength and courage." We pray that we might be shared with others through our hospitality and our work and our communion with family and friends and associates and strangers along the way. "Send us forth to do the work that You have given us to do," we pray, with all the hope and courage and joy and confidence that we can muster.

Taken, blessed, broken, shared is the essential pattern of the prayer of the Eucharist, and the essential pattern for the life of the spirit. In all places, in all times, in all things, we are at some stage of that pattern. It is the pattern that makes us whole, makes us one with Christ and each other, makes it possible for us to become a reasonable and lively sacrifice. It is the sustaining Dance of life itself.

It is a part of the Dance that we can choose to acknowledge or not. But whether or not we do so, it will overtake us in some moment and make itself known in our lives regardless of whether we ever can, or do, name it. "Those who seek to avoid suffering," wrote Merton, "are the ones who end up suffering the most. They are troubled by every little thing as well, even as they move inexorably to the suffering that is to come."

To be broken is to begin to pray the prayer of the Eucharist, "not only with our lips, but in our lives," as the old prayer says. To be broken is to begin to live the reality of the Body and Blood. To be broken is to begin to discover what they mean when they say to all the children who kneel at the table, "This is a gift from Jesus. Take it and remember that He loves you."

Planting Sweet Peas

Grant us, LORD, not to be anxious about earthly things,
but to love things heavenly; and even now,
while we are placed among things that are passing away,
to hold fast to those that shall endure.

—From THE PROPERS FOR PENTECOST

Throughout the year, the entire mystery of Christ is unfolded . . . so that
[these mysteries] of redemption are in some way present at all times,
and the faithful are enabled to lay hold of them.

—On THE CHURCH CALENDAR

The hope is for fullness, for completion,
for being one with each other. . . .
Our entire lives are a vigil,
a keeping watch, for the fulfillment of this hope.

—WENDY WRIGHT

ON VALENTINE'S DAY AT OUR HOUSE, we plant sweet peas. Sometimes we have to brush the snow away to do it, but we do it just the same. My grandmother says that no matter what the gardening books say, Saint Valentine's is the day to plant sweet peas in Tennessee if you want your sweet peas to bloom in May, and we do, and so we do.

By the time we plant sweet peas I am so sick of winter and ready for spring that I can barely be civil. The long darkness of winter always gets me down, every year, no matter what I say or do. A girl I know calls it "waiting for lamb season," as in waiting for the season that comes after March comes roaring in like a lion.

When March does finally come, we watch basketball on television—March Madness, the NCAA basketball tournament. For drama and excitement, nothing on earth, to my mind, can touch it. It is even better to me than the Olympics, partly because it comes every year, and partly because there are no equestrian events. In the early rounds of the tournament, when there is more than one game on at a time, we go to a local restaurant where they have three television sets and we watch them all simultaneously. The bartender there knows us, and he knows who we root for generally, and he waves at us every year when we come in, with our copy of *USA Today* with the tournament brackets all filled in and marked up.

When the champion is crowned, it is time for me to mow the lawn for the first time of the year. The proximity of that date to April Fool's Day crosses my mind every time I get the mower out for the first cutting. It is also time to pull off the winter mulch and reset the sprinkler hose through the border and the kitchen garden. It is seed packet month, and there are seeds arriving in our mailbox almost every day. We get out our garden journals and our charts and the little sketches of new beds and such that we dreamed up over the winter. We put sweaters on and eat supper in the yard and watch the birds scurrying through the hedges, all of us glad that the earth is turning green again.

When Cecile shows up, then it is summer, whether the calendar says so or not. Cecile Brunner is a rambling rose that is planted in the wrong place in our yard but does not seem to care. She has worked her way up a corner of the house and into a plum tree. One morning you come outside to have your coffee and there are roses blooming some thirty feet above you in the plum tree and it is May and it is summer. Then you go and sit down by Saint Francis, who stands in the white garden just in front of the iris bed, and whisper to him that it is time. The next day, it seems, the border in the lower garden is in full regalia—coreopsis and viola and violets and spiderwort, yellow and white and blue and purple. It is the best day of the year so far, and it is time to pack for Chicago.

Chicago is one of my favorite places to visit. I used to live there and so I know the city pretty well, and June is the best time to go. We go every year because there are booksellers' shows that we attend because of the work we do. For about ten days we wander through an enormous bazaar of books—free if you know how to ask for them. There are forty thousand other book people there—people who write them, read them, publish them, sell them, collect them, and love them. If there is not a book fair in heaven, then I am not going, or at least I am going to need a leave of absence every year in early June. In the late afternoons, we wander the city until it is time for wine and dinner and laughter and storytelling with all the book people that we have not seen since last year. Chicago is the first book show of the season, and when the last exhibit is closed at the last show, we go home and it is July and the children are waiting, usually in their bathing suits.

I have two young children who live in the same town but not the same house as I do. I see them every week and talk to them on the telephone almost every day, but in July they come for a long visit. Then it is time to go to the YMCA pool every day and to the beach for as long as we can afford, and to play baseball and cards and eat peanut butter and jelly and set up the lemonade stand they run off and on in our yard. When the kids go home, the grass turns brown, and it is August and time to think only about baseball.

It is too hot to do anything else in Nashville during August. So we buy *Baseball Weekly* each week and see a game or two on television when we can, and check the papers all the time so we can keep up with the pennant races. We go to the local minor league park to see a game or two, and if the young professionals are on the road, then we go over the hill to the Civitan Park, where we can still see real baseball, the kind played by the young dreamers, baseball played for love and cheers and a snow cone whether you win or lose, and a trophy to cry over some day in your thirties when you come across it in your mother's attic. One morning you hear Denise out at the corner, and it is September and it is time to go back to work.

Teachers, of course, go back to work in September, which is what accounts for my hearing Denise. She is the school crossing guard in our neighborhood and her post is at the four-way stop in front of our house. Everyone who drives by, it seems, was either a student or a parent or both who counted on her to wave them through the intersection every morning and every afternoon sometime during the past fifteen years or so. When I hear her voice, then it is time for me to go back to work too.

I consider myself a student of sorts, so I keep their hours. I write from September to May, five days a week. I even take a nap every afternoon, preferring the kindergarten plan to the middle school plan. I look forward to school supplies day every year, when I get to buy new paper and pencils and erasers. Like all students, I am just getting settled into the routine again and it is time for the World Series. October is upon us, and with it comes my favorite week of the year.

My wife and I got married on the most beautiful October day in the history of the universe. Afterward we went to the beach to celebrate. We spent the night on the road on the way to Carolina and celebrated our wedding while sharing spare champagne and cold chicken from the reception and watching Joe Carter hit a home run to win the Series. Our anniversary gift to each other each year is the gift of time. The two of us, just the two of us, go to the beach in time for our anniversary and for the World Series. When we get home, it is November and there is a telephone message from George waiting for us.

George is one of three new brothers I inherited when I got married. Of all the brothers and sisters, he is the only one who still lives in Mississippi near the old home place. About two weeks before Thanksgiving he starts laying in groceries and then he starts cooking. Then he calls everyone to see if they might like to come for dinner on Thanksgiving. He always acts as though it is the first time he ever thought of it, and we always act surprised, and almost everyone just happens to have the day free and comes for dinner. We eat too much and drink too much and laugh more than our fair share for about twelve hours. If the weather is warm we take a boat ride. If it is cold we huddle around the woodstove. Either way we stay until dark so that we can watch the barges come around the bend and glide past, all lit up with searchlights blazing away in search of the channel marker that sits a few feet from the balcony rail. When we get back home, there are RSVPs in the mailbox and that is how we know that December is upon us.

We like to hold a tea at our house at the beginning of Advent each year. My wife makes two or three of her near-legendary trifles and we decorate the house for the holidays, and set out the dessert china we found at a jumble sale and use only for this one occasion, and our friends drop by for a few minutes and stay until midnight. The candles burn and the champagne sparkles and the smiles glow and the vigil for the coming of the Light of the world begins in earnest at our house that very afternoon. Before we know it, the holiday trips are all taken, the gifts are all exchanged, the children are all surprised, the masses are all attended, and the weather turns cool. When it gets cold here, it is January.

It gets so cold in our old house that sometimes I

am willing to share the bed with the cats, just to stay warm. We read all of the books we got for Christmas, and we begin to work our way through the seed catalogs and dream of the spring and of being outside. The only joy there is on some days comes from watching the birds at the feeders that we fill every day in the hope that they will come back to live in our yard if spring ever comes again.

One day I wake up in the dark and cold of the early morning and it is time to plant sweet peas. We always plant sweet peas on Valentine's Day at our house; my grandmother told us to.

Are there not such cycles in your life? Take a week or a day or a month or a year apart and look at the twists and turns. Are there not patterns there—some delightful and some difficult, some hopeful and some discouraging, some light and some dark?

It is true of the life of prayer as well. In some ways it is a journey that is without a destination; we have already arrived all the time. The only real question does not have to do with whether or not we will get anywhere, it has to do with whether or not we are willing to acknowledge that we are somewhere already.

It is a journey upon which we embark for the sole purpose of landing at the starting point again and again. Only more aware of and more present to, more astonished and humbled and delighted by our arrival than we were the last time we noticed that we were home.

Progress, if such a practical term can be used, is measured not by the amount of ground that is covered; it is measured by the amount of attention that is paid. We must pay attention to the seasons that surround us and we must live the season in which we find ourselves.

We can drive to George's cabin in May, but no one else will be there. We can have an Advent tea in July, but no one will come. We can plant sweet peas in October, but there will be no flowers come spring.

"Whenever you do this," we are told that Jesus said to His friends at dinner one evening, "do it for the remembrance of me."

Do what in remembrance? is what I always wonder when I hear those words He said to those who would follow Him. When we gather with friends, visit our cousins, eat and drink, keep a feast day, or throw a dinner party? And when was He talking about?

Whenever we mark the seasons with celebration or sit around talking and telling stories and cleaning up the last bits of a meal? Whenever we are uncertain and afraid about what will come the next morning, or are glad to be with those we are with, or are puzzled by what someone has said in a whisper to one who sits a few places down the table, the one who mysteriously got up and left early without saying goodbye to the rest of us? We might well be remembering Him all the time then. But then what else might be the object of a life of prayer?

Why is it that we tell the story of the Nativity every year, the story that we all know by heart? It is not as though we do not know how the story goes. Why is it that we have not celebrated Easter once and for all? It is not as if we do not know how the story ends. What is there about such things that makes them worth celebrating over and over again, season after season, year after year?

"Grant us, LORD, not to be anxious . . . even now, while we are placed among things that are passing away . . ." says the prayer book, in the prayers for the season that comes as the autumn comes and the days grow shorter. The leaves die and fall and scatter before the wind that seems to get colder and colder each day. Each day we live more of our day in darkness than we do in light.

The darkness is coming in the liturgical calendar too, the part of the Story that tells of the long silence of God, the time when no prophetic voices were heard in the land, the time when it seemed certain that God's own children had been forgotten and forsaken.

"Stir up your power, O LORD, and with great might come among us . . ." we pray. Advent begins, and with it comes the far-off rumbling of something new and astonishing to be born among us. "I am about to do something new," God says to us through Isaiah as we wait in the silence and in the dark. "Can you not perceive it?" We hardly have the strength to even wonder about it, yet still we go, as Yeats said, "slouching towards Bethlehem" in the dark once again, carrying very little in our hearts to give us hope, save the promise of One Who is to Come, a Light to enlighten us all. We light our Advent candles, one more each week, saving one in expectation for the day when the Light does arrive. The darkness need not be cursed, it is the harbinger of the Light.

"You have caused this holy night to shine with

the brightness of the true Light . . . You have given Your Son to be born this day," we pray in wonder. Christmas is upon us and we discover that this new thing that we could not perceive is a child like us. It is enough to send us all dancing and singing into the streets every year, sending greetings to strangers and giving money to the poor and offering gifts to those we love. The Light itself has come and we feel compelled to do our part to honor it and make it shine just as much and for as long as we can.

"Grant that this Light," we pray, "may shine forth in our lives. . . ." The calendar says Epiphany, and we too seek and follow the Star. Stories are read of Jesus as He walked among us. For a time, it seems, we find ourselves seeing Him whenever and wherever we turn. We catch ourselves looking and listening for signs of the kingdom come. "Lead us," we pray, "we who know You by faith, to Your presence, where we may see Your glory face-to-face."

Then Lent begins and we begin to hear again that it will soon be time for the cross, that He will not always be among us in just this way, that there is a sacrifice to be made. We remember that we are to make the journey with Him, that Lent will bring us to the cross as well. "Grant that we may walk in the way of

His suffering," we pray, "that we may gladly suffer. . . ."

We find ourselves among the crowd that sings hosannas at the city gates and then among the crowd that asks for Barabbas. We see ourselves as we all too often really are and we wonder at how we could change so much and so quickly, and like His first friends, huddled in fear in a little room in the city, we are no longer sure what is to become of us.

We gather for a sad and solemn supper on a Thursday called Maundy and are fed a meal that is like no other, and we pray that "we may receive it thankfully in remembrance of Jesus, who in these holy mysteries gives us a pledge of eternal life," a pledge that is still mysterious nearly two thousand such Thursdays later.

On Good Friday we watch as the cross is draped in black and carried in silence from the sanctuary. There is no music playing when we leave on this day, no benediction or blessing ringing in our ears, only silence and the sound of our footsteps as we follow the cross out into the daylight, daylight that now seems harsh and mocking.

Sunday comes and we hear the news: He is alive and now we can be too, again, and for all time. "We thank You, heavenly Father, that You have delivered us . . . open the eyes of our faith, that we may behold Your Son in all His redeeming work. . . ." We pass Eastertide with great joy and alleluias all around, the birds and the trees and the greening of the earth accepting our song of praise alongside theirs.

The Sunday of the Ascension comes and the Christ who has walked among us is gone as He had come—powerfully, mysteriously, quickly. "Mercifully," we pray, "give us faith to believe that He will keep His promise to abide with us, that He will not leave us comfortless, but send your Holy Spirit to strengthen us. . . ."

The Spirit is indeed given to us at Pentecost, and we are sent forth with songs of triumph ringing in our ears and the Good News on our lips and the hope of the kingdom in our hearts. But the summer passes and the memories fade and Ordinary Time comes and goes and we find ourselves in the darkness and silence again. Finally the sound of the prophet is heard: "Behold, I am about to do something new. Can you not perceive it?" Once again we sit in the darkness and we light our candles and hope our hopes, and we wait for the Light of the world to come.

.   .   .

The Story that is told, over and over and over, by the liturgical calendar can open our hearts and minds and ears to our own story if we will listen. It will teach us that there will be times for us when our prayer will be that of those who live in darkness and times when it will be that of those who live in the light.

Ordinary Time seems to come to me ahead of schedule some years. Or perhaps it is Lent in my heart even when I am at the beach, and confession and penance and sacrifice are needed and loom just ahead. Sometimes even in spring, when the whole earth sings praises, the time that I spend in prayer seems dry and dead and lifeless to me.

I have a friend who is a priest who asks the same first question whenever we talk. "What dwells in you this day?" he always asks.

"Darkness, Father," I have been known to answer. "Lent, silence, fear," I might add. He smiles whenever he hears me say such things.

He smiles because he knows that I all too often forget the Story that the calendar tells and the promise that it holds—that the Coming of the Light always follows the arrival of the dark. That resurrection always follows death. That Sunday always comes after Good Friday.

If I ask him to, he will remind me that I will not

be left alone forever in the dark, that the circle will come around again, that there will be alleluias again. The truth is always this: If I will pay attention and be faithful, if I will live the seasons as they come, I will see some new thing that will be born, even in me, even if I cannot yet perceive it.

In the meantime, I will plant sweet peas on Saint Valentine's Day, even if I have to brush the snow away to do it.

Office Hours

In You we live and move and have our being:
We humbly pray that You will guide us
so that in all the cares and occupations of our life
we may not forget You.

—From THE PRAYER FOR GUIDANCE

By tradition going back to early Christian times, the divine office is
arranged so that the whole course of the day and night is made holy . . .
it is the very prayer which Christ Himself, together with His body,
addresses to the Father.

—On THE LITURGY OF THE HOURS

Things are so serious now—and values so completely cockeyed—that it
seems to me a matter of the highest moment to get even one individual
to make one more act of his free will, directing it to God in love and
faith. . . . Everything—the whole history of our world—is hanging
on such acts.

—THOMAS MERTON

THE DAY THAT I FIRST DROVE BACK into the hills of Kentucky to visit the Abbey of Gethsemani, it was cold and rainy and dreary. We spent a little time looking around, though there is not much to see if you are just stopping by. You have to be a guest retreatant at the very least to get inside the cloistered areas, and I was only there to have a look while I was passing through.

I had read some of Thomas Merton's work— he lived at Gethsemani—and I had some bit of knowledge about the life that went on behind those walls. Enough so that my imagination was working pretty hard as I listened to the Vespers bell being rung and watched the monks come scurrying from all over the farm toward the church. We had decided to stay for prayers and found ourselves a place up in the guest balcony that overlooked the monks' choir. I never saw a more ordinary group of men in my entire life. No one's face glowed, no grand current of electricity ran through the place, no thunder crashed, no angels sang.

It was just a roomful of ordinary men. Some with dirt under their fingernails and ink stains on their hands from the work they had set aside when the bell rang. Some with orthopedic shoes and some with cross-trainers and some with sandals. Some had glasses and some looked young enough to be my own son. One or two looked bored to tears, one had a terrible voice, and a couple were sort of breathless, as though they had run the last few yards to arrive in their stall before the loud knock that signaled the beginning of the prayer. There might have been a hall monitor for all I know.

Oh, it was beautiful all right, breathtakingly so. The sound of those voices in unison, chanting the words of prayers that had been prayed and sung by the faithful for centuries. The flickering of candlelight against the whitewashed walls. The vast silence of the sanctuary, with its shadows and its light and its clean lines and its stark empty spaces. The nobility and simplicity of these faithful men arrested our spirits for a while, carrying us into the quiet presence of God.

But if one of the monks was transported into some grand and transcendent experience down there among them, I never saw it. The community simply stopped its work, gathered to pray, and dispersed, going on to the next part of the day, letting the act and the art of their prayer speak for itself. They simply made their offering and went back to work. It seemed simply a part of the life that they live, something done not with great flourish or emotion but with great devotion and faithfulness. There was a blessed ordinariness to it.

When it was over, and it was over too soon for me, it was time to go back to work. The monks started out the door to theirs and we went down the stairs and out the door toward the parking lot, where the car was waiting to take me back to mine.

In the society in which we live, the primary rule of work seems to be to cram as much into the hours of the day as you can. The longer you work and the more exhausted you are, the more status you seem to have. Nobody wants to admit that they are so unimportant that they do not have to come in on Saturdays just to keep up with their mail. If you can have a car phone and a home fax and a beeper so that any client or customer or boss or employee can get hold of you anytime, anywhere, for anything, then you really are something.

We have power breakfasts, business lunches, and

client dinners. We even take working vacations, a term whose meaning escapes me somehow. If you ask people how they are doing, they will say good or bad depending on how their work is going, regardless of whether or not their marriage is failing or their kids are in trouble or their house is on fire. Sometimes you think you can see it enter someone's mind to say something other than, "Great, fine, really good," but then they hold back. They assume that since they do not want to think about it, then you could not possibly really want to hear about it either.

I can remember conversations around an office water cooler in which we all preened in front of each other by bragging about how late we got home or how early we had come in or how many days we had been on the road this month. It was silly and childish, like little boys making up lies about their fathers to impress their friends. Like those easily spoken lies, the desperation in the truth that they seek to cover is terrible and painful.

We take our place in the race and watch our lives disappear in the daily grind. We rush through the present toward some future that is supposed to be better but generally turns out only to be busier. We hurry through our prayers and miss them—just as we race through our meals and do not linger over the coffee and conversation. We crash our children out the door in the morning so we can get on to the real world.

"Be careful what you treasure . . ." I read somewhere once. I do not think about it much; my treasure shows itself all too clearly.

Our work has become almost everything to us. Our lives are built around it and the fruits of it. Productivity, success, efficiency have become the watchwords of the day. It is no wonder that our days seem very often to be devoid of meaning. At best, they are built around about a fourth of who we are. It is not necessarily the work itself that is killing us, it is the way we give it such meaning and power and control over our lives.

Our lives hang in the balance, one might say. And if there is no balance, then they are indeed hanging by a thread.

I stood on the steps outside the chapel at Gethsemani and watched as other guests filed out. I watched as a monk or two came out as well, some task calling them from within the enclosure for a while. I was trying to think contemplative thoughts, trying to savor the sense and spirit of the moment, when a monk went past me and knelt down and began to pull weeds from a flower bed. Over to my left, across the hill, I saw three monks with big heavy boots on and shovels over their shoulders heading for the fields across the way. They were giggling. Through a window I caught a glimpse of a monk carrying linens and cleaning supplies down the hall of the guest house. I heard a door slam and a tractor start up. Then I saw two monks come out the front door with briefcases and climb into the back seat of a car that had out-of-state license plates and two rather distinguished-looking people inside in the front seat.

I started laughing to myself because it occurred to me that somewhere behind those walls someone was setting the table and sorting the mail and filling cheese orders. Somebody was balancing a checkbook and somebody was cooking supper and somebody was making a grocery list. Somebody had bad news from home and somebody's brother was coming to visit and somebody was getting transferred and could hardly wait. Somebody had just gotten a promotion and somebody was peeved about a job he had been assigned and somebody was looking forward to being on retreat for a few days, so he could slow down and rest from the daily grind.

The lives of the monks of Gethsemani are very different from mine. But the difference has less to do with celibacy and fashion and location, and everything to do with what happens when the bell rings.

When the bell rings, they pray. Everything is different because of that one thing.

At the Academy, the rule was that you could not eat until you had prayed. I do not mean you had to wait on someone to say grace, I mean they did not open the dining room until after morning prayers had been said. You could not complain about it either, because you could not break the Great Silence that was observed between the close of night prayers and the beginning of morning prayers each day.

Everything there was like that. Every day the work and the rest and the study and the meals were built around the prayer of the community. The prayer marked the hours and the tasks and the pace of each day. It framed the movements of the day itself.

You simply could not do anything until you had participated in the prayer that sanctified the day. After a while, you did not want to; the prayer came first, even in your own mind.

The basic structure for the Academy day was lifted from the monastic tradition of Saint Benedict, the same tradition followed by the monks of Gethsemani. In a monastic community the object is to learn to pray without ceasing. Saint Benedict figured out that even monks had to eat to stay alive, and had to work to eat, and had to study to learn to pray, and had to have time for rest and for showing hospitality to those who were among them, whether they came as guests or as pilgrims in need or fellow members of the community.

The Rule of Saint Benedict was formed as a way of shaping a day in the life of a community that would balance and harmonize the community's needs and responsibilities for prayer, work, study, and rest. It looked like any other community's day—eat, work, eat, work, eat, rest—except for that one other activity: pray.

It is the prayer that gives the day its shape and form and creates balance and harmony. All other parts of the Rule—rest, community, work—are placed on the foundation and within the framework of the prayer itself.

A fair portion of the things that make the community at Gethsemani seem so different from the one you and I live in is simply made up of traditions and habits that are reasonable and proper to make their way of life possible. But those things are no better or worse, no holier or unholier, than some of the things that are reasonable parts of running any household so that there is order and harmony and things get done in a way that allows people to be who they are and do what they have been called to do. Which is what I hope happens at my house. We too have rules and traditions and habits that bring some order and some possibility for becoming and being who we are. The biggest difference is that when the bell rings, the monks pray. Their common life, and the Rule that governs it, starts with prayer and then the other things—work, community, rest—are added as they are needed and desired, and can be balanced.

What struck me that morning in Kentucky, oddly enough, was not how different my life had to be from that of these men of prayer, but how much our lives could be alike.

They have a vocation and so do I. They have taken a vow of stability and so have I (or at least my wife and children certainly think so). They have chores to do and so do I. They have work to do and so do I. They have people they live with and people who come to visit and so do I. They dress funny, and some would say, so do I. They have taken seriously Paul's admonition to pray without ceasing and so . . . so could I . . . if. . . .

If what? What holds me back? Why could I not live a life framed by prayer? Because I was not called to be a monk? Or because I will not answer the bell?

The daily prayer of the Church is called by many names—the daily office, the divine office, the hours, the liturgy of the hours. But whatever name you use, what it is meant to be is this: the prayer of the Body of Christ that sanctifies each day. It has its roots in the ancient Hebrew traditions and was shaped and refined in the desert with the ammas and the abbas. It can be found in similar forms throughout Catholic and Orthodox communities, and throughout many of the more liturgical traditions in the Protestant world.

It is the prayer of the prayer books, prayer that is often castigated as being rote and mechanical, as being dry and without life, as being only for monks and nuns and priests and clerics. It is prayer that is mysterious and far away somehow. Its various parts are called by names like Prime and Matins and Lauds, names we do not know and are not familiar with. It is full of collects and responses and observances of saints' days and other things that we do not know much about.

Such prayer seems anachronistic and complicated and not nearly as real to us as the kind of vocal prayer that we most often think of when we think of prayer. But this prayer that we know so little about is in fact the kind of prayer that can shape the way we live our days so that they become something more real than the days we seem to live now. It is prayer that will not let you forget why you were made and for Whom. It is prayer that will not let you live your life without paying attention. It is prayer that is not dependent on your intellect or emotion or eloquence. It primarily calls for devotion and faithfulness.

The words and themes of the prayers—creation, calling, vocation, intercession, rest, confession, death, resurrection—remind us that each day is whole unto itself. The rhythm of the prayer creates and allows for the beginning and the ending of separate parts of the day, a natural ebb and flow that mirrors the light and

the dark, the sun and the shadow of a day, a week,
a life.

In a day's prayer one practices contemplative
prayer, intercessory prayer, sacred reading, confession,
praise, silence—the various habits of the heart that
can help one pay attention for the Voice that we can
hear "if we will but listen for His voice," as the
psalmist urges in the Venite at morning prayers. The
dependence on and adherence to the structure and
language—the psalms, the canticles, the propers, the
collects, the responses, the litanies—provide language
and focus and rhyme and reason when such things are
hard to come by because of our circumstances. They
provide the focus needed to keep one's prayer from
becoming self-centered and myopic.

The daily office is the prayer that can provide a
frame for the day that both shapes and reflects our
lives and the way they are to be lived. Such prayer
connects us with the ancient traditions and practices
that have been used by many of the saints and
pilgrims who have walked this way before.

The next time I went to Gethsemani, the weather was
better and so I walked across the road and up a hill

that allows a view down to and over the monastery walls. It was quiet and peaceful and warm in those rolling Kentucky hills that day.

I could see monks going here and there from time to time. I saw one on a tractor mowing a field, the way I used to when I was a kid. He sang to himself too, just the way I did.

From the top of the hill, I could hear the bells ring in the tower above the cloister. When certain bells rang, I could see monks moving across the fields or through the courtyard in the direction of the church. It was time to pray.

"The bells," writes Merton, "break in upon our cares in order to remind us that all things pass away and that our preoccupations are not important. . . . The bells say: business does not matter."

I hear no church bells in my neighborhood, though on a quiet day, if the wind is just right, I can hear the school bell from the elementary school down the street. I think that the closest church bell to our neighborhood is six or seven miles back down the road toward town. If I want a bell to call me to something, I am going to have to set my alarm or the little beeper on my computer screen or something.

"The bells say: we have spoken for centuries from

the towers of great Churches," Merton goes on. "We have spoken to the saints, your fathers, in their land. We called them, as we call you, to sanctity."

We too are called to sanctity. We too are called to participate in the prayer that indeed brings sanctity to the day. We who have no robes and no bell towers to remind us. We who live surrounded by shopping malls rather than grain fields. We too belong to God, we too are the Body of Christ, and we too must pray His prayer in the world into which we have been called.

The call to the monastery is given only to a few. The call to prayer is given to all.

A man once asked the Vietnamese monk Thich Nhat Hanh what it is that monks actually do. "We walk and we sit and we eat," was the reply.

"Is that all?"

"Yes. But when we walk, we know we are walking, and when we sit, we know we are sitting, and when we eat, we know we are eating."

Which is more than most of us can say we know most of the time. Most of the time, we are somewhere in the past or the future. The past echoes and the future beckons; the present just seems to be sitting on the edge of the bed leering at us when we wake up in the morning. It does not always seem like much, so we do not often pay it much mind. When we do visit the present from time to time, we are likely to wonder why it is not what it seems like it used to be or not what we had hoped it might be. We rarely are content to live in it just the way it is.

"There is only now," wrote Merton.

The daily prayer of the faithful can create places in our hearts and minds that can be filled with something besides worry and fear about the days that we can no longer live or cannot yet reach.

"God said, 'Let there be light,' and there was light," we pray as the dawn begins to break. "This very day the LORD has acted." The morning light is upon us, God having chosen again to give us light and life. The world is created anew each morning, an Eden for us to explore, a garden in which to wander and wonder. It is good to get up early to see it fresh with the dew; God does much of His best work around sunrise.

"We praise You with joy, loving God, for Your grace is better than life itself. You have sustained us through the darkness and You have blessed us with life in this new day." We give our thanks, acknowledging the One Who gives all gifts. We see the trees around us, stark and silent with winter, bright and lush come the spring, bursting with blooms and blossoms in summer, brilliant and breathtaking with autumn. We see our homes around us, our families, our children, our lovers, our friends, the ones to whom we have been given again this day. Grateful is a better way to begin our day than with only the worry and weariness of the burdens to be borne.

"Guide our feet into the paths of peace, that having done Your will this day, we may, when night comes, rejoice and give You thanks. . . ." We begin the work that is before us this day, asking for the grace to do it well and to the glory of God. We dress children and get them to school, we find our places and undertake the tasks for which we have been dreamed into being. We do the work that is before us, the gift of study or play, the tasks and assignments, the places to go and the people to see. We begin to sense that our work can be changed from job and task into service and act of kindness, from the struggle for gain into the offering of gift, from slow death into life-giving co-creation. The work itself can become something more as we come to see ourselves as co-laborers rather than pawns, as the hands and feet of God rather than merely the shoulders and backs of the marketplace. We keep our eyes open for the One Who Comes among us in our daily rounds.

The sun moves across the sky until it is overhead. Somewhere perhaps a bell rings, the streets are filled, a break is called for. We stop for a while to feed our bodies, and our spirits cry out for refreshment as well.

"Deliver us from the service of self alone," we pray, "that we may do the work You have given us to do, in truth and beauty and for the common good, for the sake of the One Who Comes among us as One Who serves." The daily round begins to move toward its close, and the shadows grow. In our hearts and hands we hold the remnants of the day, the things accomplished and the things left undone. In our memories are the faces and words and acts and voices of those with whom we have shared this day—the joyous and the sad, the blessed and the broken, the peacemakers and the troublemakers, the afflicted and the comfortable. We look for closure to the day, for forgiveness and reconciliation and peace at the last.

"Yours is the morning and Yours is the evening. Draw us near to You, so there will be no darkness in us. You have made this day for the works of the light and this night for the refreshment of our minds and our bodies. . . ." Home. Oh, what we have seen and heard this day, the mercies and the graces, the pain and the suffering, the names and the faces, the Christ and the Crucified. We break bread, we kiss our kids, we hold our spouse, we visit friends, we watch the ballet or the news or the game, or the sun set and the moon rise.

"You have been our help during the day and You have promised to be with us at night. Receive this prayer as a sign of our trust in You. . . ." The house begins to grow quiet and still. The darkness begins to cover us too, slowly, surely, irrevocably.

"We confess that we have sinned against You this day. . . . In the name of Christ, we ask forgiveness. Deliver and restore us that we may rest in peace." We pray that our sins will sleep as we do, but that, through the mercy of the One Who moves in the darkness and the deep, they never awaken. "Let your servant now depart in peace as You have promised. . . ."

This day is done. We are entered once again into the world of darkness and of dreams, a world without form and void. God's whole creation, or at least our corner of it, has been born and has lived, has been reconciled and completed. It is finished. "Into Your hands we commend our spirits," we pray. And sometime in the night, in the darkness, in the Great Silence itself, the God Who never slumbers and never sleeps begins to whisper out into the void again.

Our eyes open slowly and we listen to the creaking of the stars and the groaning of the world, half expecting to hear the sound of the angels, perhaps even the rocks and the stones themselves crying out. We can hear the sound of our hearts beating to the song of creation. "God said, 'Let there be light. . . .' This very day. . . . Rejoice."

I have begun to learn that without the prayers themselves, without the structure and frame and rhythm they provide, the hours and the days all too quickly begin to run together. Again and again, the time goes by too fast, the work mounts up and overwhelms, nothing is ever finished. God's time, sanctified time, is different from ours.

In God's time, there is completion to this day in which the LORD has acted: one is created, works as one is called, intercedes as one can, listens as one is able, confesses the gap between who one was created to be and who one is, commits one's spirit to the One Who gave it, and lies down in peace to die, in the hope of a resurrection, if not later then sooner, in the morning perhaps.

If nothing else, the meager attempts that I have made to live within the steps of this Ancient Dance have brought to me the gift of having a way at least in which a day can be sanctified and made holy. It need not be lived for any more or less than it is meant to be. It is lived in the present, not the past or the future.

The offices are not always easy to pray. They are certainly not always convenient. It is harder to pray such prayer alone than it is with others, and yet finding others with whom to pray the offices is not easy at all.

But they can be prayed; we can participate in the prayer of the Body of Christ that sanctifies the day. It takes faith and devotion. It will require that we give ourselves up to its process, and to the way it has of beginning to reshape our lives and the way we live them.

It will cost time and energy, though not so much of either as we might think. We do not have to invent it each day, nor is it dependent on our eloquence. It can be read from books and allowed to be turned loose in the world to do its work even when we do not understand or enjoy it.

It is prayer that can change us, make no mistake about it. The changes may go unnoticed for a long time, but they will come.

It will change the way we see our work and our rest. It will change the way we live with others. It will slowly, inexorably draw us into itself and unto the One for Whom and by Whom it is prayed, and into the sanctity of the days that have been given to us and to which we have been given.

The Road Leads Here

You have taught us
that in returning and rest we shall be saved,
in quietness and confidence we shall be strengthened:
By Your Spirit lift us to Your presence,
where we may be still and know that You are God.

—From THE PRAYER FOR
QUIET CONFIDENCE

Solitude has always been considered a means of achieving
greater union with God . . . a basis for the retreats made by [those] who
seek some communication with God through prayer and meditation.

—On SOLITUDE

The real in us is silent; the acquired is talkative.

—KAHLIL GIBRAN

THERE SEEMS TO BE A CLOCK THAT GOES OFF in my head about every seventy-five or eighty days or so. For much of my life I did not even know that it was there.

It is a close cousin, I think, to the clock that goes off in me twice a year telling me it is time to go to the beach. I learned about that internal clock pretty early. My father had one too, and so I got a fair amount of practice when I was growing up in the art of paying attention to the beach clock. In fact, I can tell you now that it will go off in July and October next year. I am so certain that I even made reservations already.

But this other clock was one that I did not know about for a long time. It is the one, I have come to discover, that calls me to silence and to solitude and to retreat.

Which is how I found myself on the road to Sumatanga, headed for the Academy for Spiritual Formation.

Sumatanga is not too hard to find, provided you

know how to find Gallant, Alabama. Which is simple, of course. You just leave the interstate highway at Reece City, go to Attalla, cross the highway that leads to Birmingham and points south (I think) and then on into Gallant. At least, the people who gave me directions told me that it was simple. In two years, I made eight trips down and eight trips back and got lost six times.

Gallant is not exactly the end of the line, but when the light is good, you can see it from there. When you get to "town," ask someone at the store how to find Sumatanga. You may not even have to ask. Except for people who live there, all six hundred and thirty of them, or people who are headed to Sumatanga, nobody else goes through Gallant much. If they do not know you, they know where you are headed. A man answered the question for me before I could get it out of my mouth.

Sumatanga is this great rambling Methodist campground that has grown topsy-turvy over the years. It has a main lodge and a chapel in the woods, a youth camp where there is a swimming pool surrounded by plenty of woods to keep the grown-ups in their place, a tennis court and a lake, and hiking trails and pine trees. It sits hard by the foot of what passes for a mountain in this part of the world, and a stream cuts through the woods in the space between the mountain and the lodge and empties into the little lake. It is beautiful and quiet and restful.

There is a trail to the top of the mountain. When you get to the top, there is a dirt road that runs across the ridge. If you go left a mile or so, you will find an open-air stone chapel that looks down on the lake and the lodge and the valley below. If you go right, you will come to a huge, electrified cross that can be seen at night for miles around, except that no one lives in the miles around. But I expect that pilots passing overhead have seen it.

The first trip I made to Sumatanga, I arrived about three hours ahead of time. I do not generally arrive anywhere so early, and no one was there. Had anyone been there I would not have known what to say anyway. I have no idea what to say when you are early. I am well aware of what to say when you are late. I have plenty of experience at that.

I was so anxious to be there I had actually packed my things about three days before. I have a clear memory of having unpacked my gear twice, on two separate evenings no less, to make sure that I had everything I would need. It reminded me of how excited I had been when I was a kid and headed off to basketball camp for the first time.

After I arrived, I took a walk, trying to get the lay of the land and to calm down. As the others began to turn up, I sat out on the stone steps across from the lodge and watched them gather. There was a fair amount of hugging and carrying on among all the Alabamans who knew each other, of course, and after a while it seemed to me that even the non-Alabamans, having shared rides or airport shuttles or seminary professors, were soon being slapped on the back and chatted up as though they had been around for years.

I sort of kept my eye out for some shy ones who might break away from the group and head off by themselves where it might be safe for me to talk to them, but by and large everyone seemed to be traveling in packs. To be honest, some of them did come over and introduce themselves, which set off the kind of mumbling small-talk business I do among strangers, and though a fair number of folks cheerily attempted to get to know me that afternoon, I managed to resist all of them.

The only one who sat next to me on the steps for any length of time was a Korean fellow from

Colorado. I have come to believe that my mumbling was so bad that he thought my English was broken and he felt sorry for me. After having been his unofficial welcoming party, I was not too surprised when he dropped out later in the week and went home to Colorado. I would have too if I had to count on me to be the hospitality committee. The truth is that as the sun started to go down behind the hills, and the darkness began to creep through the trees, and the long-anticipated afternoon wore on and on, I started to feel less and less like I belonged there.

I had discovered a little chapel with a stone bench and I finally wandered over to it and wandered in and closed the door. I thought that having come all this way, the least I could do was pray some. After about fifteen minutes, I realized that I was crying a lot more than I was praying, which also reminded me of going away to basketball camp, because I cried that day too. But then I was ten at the time.

"God, I don't belong here," I sniffed. "These people all know each other and I do not know anyone. And I am no saint, just this kind of lost, shy man who is sitting out here on the steps while the chosen ones are swapping hugs and memories and stories. And this isn't the Promised Land, for Pete's sake, it's Alabama."

This sort of eloquent and scintillating prayer went on for a couple of hours actually. *Self-pitio* is the Latin term for it, I think. Before you feel too sorry for me, you should know that it was actually very cool and nice in the chapel, and I managed to completely avoid helping strangers with their luggage and the danger of getting caught up in any mixer games. "God, what am I doing in this place? Why am I here?"

Then something happened to me that I did not understand then, and understand even less now that I know the Latin, mystical, transpersonal, philosophical, theological, and psychological names for it. What happened was that I heard a Voice say something to me. I will not, cannot elaborate; it already embarrasses me in a way to say even that much. But years later I am still convinced that I heard a Voice and the Voice said to me, "You promised to follow wherever I might take you, and this is where we go next. You are here because the road leads here."

I came to Sumatanga from a life that was pretty much like everyone else's life. Up as early as you can, drag yourself out, hustle the household off to school and to work and so forth, drive downtown muttering at the traffic, work like crazy until there is just enough time to fight your way through the traffic to have a meal, watch some television, and collapse into bed, knowing that if you thought about it you could very easily go ahead and start being tired for tomorrow as well.

The way we live our lives in our cities and towns simply assaults most all of us most all of the time. The sheer unadulterated noise level is enough to make us crazy. Most of the time, we do not even notice. It has become so commonplace, so ordinary, that we are oblivious to it. Perhaps there is a contest going on that I was not told about, the prize going to the person who can tolerate the most noise.

The constant assault and agitation drains us and diminishes our spirits. We are just kind of sucked into it and it pulls the life and energy from us. We just talk louder or turn the volume up and try to keep dogging our way through it. It seems to bother some people a good deal less than it does others. A fair number of people I know claim to be able to go along for years without some measure of silence and solitude. Some of us, however, more of us than notice or care to admit, are deeply affected by the lack of quiet in our lives.

We do all manner of things to cope with the noise and the pace. We get speed-dial and VoiceMail systems and beepers and E-mail so that we can keep conversations going with dozens of people we have no time to talk to. We put phones in our cars so that we can do business while we listen to cassettes of the books we do not have the time to read, so that our daily commute from the places we moved to for peace and quiet doesn't turn into wasted time.

Every so often, a clock seems to go off in us, or a question, and we find ourselves hungry for some bit of silence and solitude and rest and quiet. But we are on the road or in a meeting or booked solid and we do not have time for it and we do not answer its call.

Since I seem to have been so ill equipped for life in the twentieth century, and to prepare myself for life in the twenty-first century, I have recently begun to develop a theory of life in our times that I call the Rule of 21.

Twenty-one minutes is the amount of time that one can go without being interrupted by a telephone call, a knock at the door, or an attack from cyberspace in one form or another.

Twenty-one days seems to be the maximum number of days that one's life can go smoothly. The average is more like four, but the limit is twenty-one, I think. It is hard to live more than twenty-one days without a car breaking down, a trip being canceled, a family member getting sick, a pet dying, a check bouncing, a tire going flat, a deadline being missed, or some other thing that scatters all of one's neatly arranged ducks.

Twenty-one weeks is the absolute maximum amount of time that I can go without some meaningful silence and solitude, or else my nerves get shaky, my work suffers, and my relationships start running on empty. That period of roughly one hundred and fifty days is about fifty percent farther than I should attempt to travel without a retreat.

I need time to listen, to examine, and to confess, time to take off some of the hats I wear. I need time to listen for the Voice, if for no other reason than so I will recognize it more clearly in the ways it speaks into the noise and bustle of the life I lead.

The silence that I seek must be nurtured until it lives in me no matter where I am at the moment. It was easy to find silence on the mountain at

Sumatanga, but what do I do now that I no longer am required to go there? How is one to hear the Voice if one cannot even hear oneself think?

The silence that I seek cannot merely be the absence of the numbing noise and debilitating detail of life in our society. It must be something more. It must be a solitude that is transcendent, a stillness that can be found in the midst of the noise, a silence that is portable.

The experience I had that afternoon in the chapel at Sumatanga was the first of several important moments that took place there over the next two years. They were more or less dramatic than that one, but they changed my life.

I remember a particular night on the mountain and the day that we revisited our baptisms. I can hear Ed and Hazelyn and Wendy and Dwight and Norman and the sentences they said that changed me irrevocably. I remember the long walks in the dark and the late evenings in the chapel in the candlelight. I could tell you all of these stories, but they hold great meaning only for me. They are important to you perhaps only because they are evidence of what happens when one surrenders to the process of going away to listen.

In the time I was there, I actually became more and more of who I actually am. I discovered more and more about the ways to which I was being drawn and the life to which I was being called. I learned more and more about the ways in which the Voice speaks to me and would do so again and again, if I would stop to listen.

And I finally have come to have a sense of the silence that can be transcendent, that can go with us into the noise and the bustle of the lives we lead.

"In the course of this busy life," we pray, "grant us times of refreshment and peace." We set a mark on our calendars and then we hit it. We take our favorite old sweater and a book that has become a teacher to us and our journals from the time since we last made a retreat, and we go away. We find a place where bells can be heard, where prayers are said every day, where silence rather than talk is the rule.

"Grant that our spirits may be opened to the goodness of Your creation." We eat when we are hungry, sleep when we are tired. We take long walks to nowhere in particular and sit on benches for hours at a time listening to birds and watching clouds. We hear ourselves breathe, we feel a breeze on our face, we sit outside in the dark and look at the stars. For a day or two, or a week, we pay no attention to watches and time clocks and telephones and traffic copters—the trappings of the society we have made. We pay attention for a time only to what God has made.

We pray that we may "so use such time to renew our minds," by letting our minds lie fallow for a time; by not engaging them every waking moment in the things that pass away. We savor the sweetness in the book that we brought, we listen between the lines to our own story again. Sometimes a wise one, a modern-day abba or amma, is there to help us listen; sometimes we are absolutely alone. Sometimes we go away with a particular question to wrestle with, sometimes we go, as Ed Farrell says, to "walk the shoreline of our own being and see what has washed up in the night."

"Source of all wisdom and understanding, be present with those who take counsel here . . ." goes the prayer. We look through our journals and see where we have been burying our treasure, our time, our love, our money. We take stock of our work and our relationships, our avocations and vocations. We mourn our losses and confess our mistakes. We give thanks for our gifts and renew our promises. We are present to our deepest selves for a time, and in doing so, discover the Truth to be found at the place where deep calls to Deep.

With our eyes wide open and our hearts quite still and our minds near empty, we pray: "Guide us to perceive what is right. . . ." We see more clearly to whom we have been given and understand more completely what is the cup of cold water that we have to offer them. We see the lines and the boundaries that must enclose our choices, we see what is most important and most precious and most holy in our lives. We sense what for us is our one true necessity and how to arrange the hours and days of our lives around just that.

"Grant us the courage to pursue these things and the grace to accomplish them," we pray as we set our faces toward home. We make a list or write a letter. We make a symbolic act: an offering at a Eucharist, a stick thrown into a fire, a leaf cast into a stream, a line drawn in the dust. We make it in silence, joining our silence to the Silence that surrounds us, so that only the Silence knows.

The time apart draws to a close and we make our journey home, back to the places and people and work to which we are given. We have offered our silence and solitude, and the offering has been taken and blessed. In return, the Silence at the center of all things—the "center to which all things tend," as Merton describes it—goes with us. Silently, compassionately, it lives and grows in our hearts amid the bustle of the life that we lead, growing its way toward a transcendence in us.

"In the course of this busy life, grant that our spirits may be opened . . ." we pray.

These days, when the retreat clock goes off, I have other places I go. My days as part of the Academy have ended and so I get lost on the way to places other than Sumatanga.

I have been to monasteries and convents, to retreat centers and hermitages, to all kinds of places. Sometimes I go with friends, sometimes alone. I am always at home in the places where silence is sought, though I am still just as shy about strangers being around, and still just as apt to worry about whether or not I am holy enough to be on the grounds.

But I belong. I belong because the Silence itself has drawn me. I belong because my hunger for prayer has brought me in search of places where nothing else matters, at least for a while. I belong to such places because the road, the road that leads to prayer, the road that I have promised to follow no matter where it leads—the road leads here.

Ink Stains on the Soul

You proclaim Your truth in every age by many voices:
Direct those, we pray, who speak where many listen
and write what many read;
that they may do their part
in making the heart of Your people wise,
its mind sound, and its will righteous.

—From THE PRAYER FOR THOSE
WHO INFLUENCE OTHERS

The question of the presence of Christ in the exterior world of facts and
institutions and in the interior world of the hearts of men is at the
center of our religion.

—On PRAYER

Always when I was without a book, my soul would at once become
disturbed, and my thoughts wandered. As I read, I began to call them
together again and, as it were, laid a bait for my soul.

—SAINT TERESA OF AVILA

As far as I am concerned, nothing that cyberspace has to offer will ever beat the smell of ink on the page or the feel of book cloth in the hands. I fully expect that when all the new communication in the world is electronic, I will be among the last twelve people or so on earth who would rather have a book. When the aforementioned sign of the apocalypse is upon us, come to my house. If there are any books left in the world, some of them will be there, and you can borrow them if you promise to bring them back.

At our house, a really good weekend is one spent in bed with a book. It is probably a holdover from the sort of wisdom that was passed on to me by my father. He was sick a lot in his life, and he maintained that you should never go to bed sick without a stack of new books. "Have books, will convalesce" was his motto.

A book can do powerful things to you if you are not careful. In *An American Childhood,* Annie Dillard notes that when she was a girl she was "always looking for something real, more real, and I could only find it in books." Me too, I think.

I read enough Hardy Boys when I was young to expect that young and dashing was going to be my basic posture all my life. I am married to a woman who maintains that she really needs only a Nancy Drew roadster to call her life complete. A match made in heaven if ever there was one.

When I was in my early twenties, I read *Working*, the classic book by Studs Terkel, and it absolutely changed for me forever the way I view work, my own and others'. One of my favorite quotes of all time is in that book and I have been quoting it from memory for twenty-five years or so. I cannot say for certain whether it is the cause or the explanation, but I have struggled with the entire notion of a regular paycheck and an office cubicle and a shot at a gold watch ever since.

My best friend grew up in church, left it for a long while, and then came back to it. She will tell you that the credit for her return to the Church lies squarely on the shoulders of Susan Howatch, whose six stunning novels about the Anglican Church are required reading every year for all adults at her house.

It is not exactly news that a person who spends

his life writing books, or trying to (some days a decent paragraph seems beyond me), would love books. It is not astonishing to think that books would have affected me so. What is surprising, to me at least, is not that they had so much to do with my writing life. It is that they have had so much to do with my praying life.

According to Robert Mulholland, a noted seminarian in the field of spiritual formation, there are two ways to read: informational reading and formational reading.

The first is the kind of reading that most of us do most all of the time. At its simplest, it is stop signs and billboards, horoscopes and headlines, and memos and magazines, the reading that we do to stay in touch with our work and our culture and our day-to-day life. We read such things for the information itself; it tells us what we need to know to keep functioning. It is also the reading that we do for entertainment or curiosity or escape, or because we are convinced that we cannot get a proper suntan without a book in our hands. We get a stack of such things in the mail or on our desk and we work through it as fast as we can, gleaning from it what we need or want, whether consciously or unconsciously. Then we put it down or pass it on and it is gone.

The other kind of reading, formational reading, is reading that is not about our working on the stuff that is written on the page, it is about the stuff on the page working on us. It is what we read in the name of looking to learn, but what we are really looking for, whether we know it or not, is to be changed. Which can happen to us at the hands of a book.

It is what happened to Annie Dillard's father. "When I was ten, my father's reading went to his head," she says in the hopes of explaining, to herself mostly, why, under the influence of Twain's *Life on the Mississippi,* her father traded his executive position for a houseboat and headed downriver from Pittsburgh to New Orleans to become a jazz musician.

Such things happen to people all the time under the influence of the written word. It is what happened to me when I read Studs Terkel. It is what happened to my friend when she read Susan Howatch. Such a thing, or something very like it, is what must have happened to Saint Teresa. Her father's books and her mother's prayers made her a nun. Having read her books, I think she might just as easily have become a novelist or a lunatic had it not been for her father's holy books.

In the traditions of prayer, you come across three terms that have to do with reading and prayer, with the mental prayer that the contemplatives teach. Mental prayer, as opposed to verbal or liturgical or communal prayer.

The first of those three terms is *lectio divina,* sacred reading. It is primarily thought of in connection with the scriptures, and in fact, that is the easiest way to understand it. It was and still is held in high enough regard to be institutionalized in certain religious communities into the Office of Readings, suggesting that one's prayer discipline is not complete each day without the disciplined reading of the scriptures and the holy writings of the mothers and fathers of the faith.

In *lectio,* you begin by reading a scripture passage slowly, aloud perhaps, once or twice or three times. Then you imagine yourself in the setting of the scripture itself. You see yourself as the different characters in the story or the setting, you listen to the sounds that emanate from it, touch its textures, smell its smells, feel its tensions. Then you begin to listen for what it is saying to you, making notes if you think to, not making notes if you do not want to. Journal against it or not. Paint pictures if you like. Or simply sit and say a phrase over to yourself, the phrase that catches your eye and quickens your heart this day. The hearing is prayer itself. The hearing is the beginning of being "shaped by the Word," as Mulholland calls it.

We are not altogether unfamiliar with such a notion. Preachers engage us in the practice quite a bit, attempting to open us up to the stories in the scriptures that they are attempting to unlock for us on a given Sunday morning. Some of us have even done a bit of it on our own, guided by our own lights or by the ones in a devotional book we picked up somewhere. This is the point at which we generally pronounce the exercise over, and offer a quick verbal prayer and head off to something else. With us we carry a sort of low-level exegesis, one that often reflects only what we already know and already believe to be true, or what is in the commentary or devotional book that we are reading, or what we know is safe, acceptable theology in the crowd we run with.

The saints suggest that there is something more, that if we stop here, we stop before we have really begun. And they have a name for what comes next if you are willing to go there.

That practice is called *meditatio,* meditation. It is here that the material you have read begins to reverse the hold. It starts to work on you rather than you on it. Your imagination begins to move along where it will, and you let it run. It wanders its way back into the details of your own life and you follow, letting yourself be taken to a place where the Word wants to take you this day. You do it with your heart rather than your mind.

The difference between the two is very subtle, but very important. It is the difference between hearing and listening, the difference between being quiet and being silent, the difference between choreography and the Dance itself.

The third stage is out beyond there somewhere. It is called *contemplatio,* contemplation. In two thousand years of devotion, even the most saintly of the saints are united on two things about it. Contemplation is the most desirable stage of prayer, and it is also the one that no one can explain very well.

It is not so much you praying to God, but God praying in you. It is not about visions and supernatural phenomena, although such things can be a part of it from time to time. It often begins with thought, conscious thought, but you cannot predictably think your way into it. It is not something that happens often, not even for the saints. It may last for a few moments or for hours, so we are told. It is a place that you cannot seek, it will come and find you. But it is the communion of the highest order that we can know here, the closest we can come to union with God.

The week that we were having all of this explained to us in the Academy, and being sent out to practice the practices a bit to see if we could begin to get the hang of it, a feisty little nun from South Dakota was one of the ones doing the teaching and the guiding. To one of us who was worried about getting all of the steps right, Sister Miriam said, "Do not worry if what you are doing is *lectio* or *meditatio* or *contemplatio*. God does not care."

I think what she was saying was that it is the process that counts, the time given, the willingness to turn the Word and the Voice loose in us. It is the willingness to listen to the scriptures and the saints and even the sound of our own innermost being, the being into which God has whispered things that no one else will ever hear.

It is the willingness to let the Word form us rather than always being content with or insisting upon what we can dig out with our own intellect and understanding.

A man I know drove by our house every day for two years on his way home from work, and one day he saw me out in the yard. He did not know that was where I lived. He pulled over to say that he had driven by every evening for two years and wondered who belonged to all those books he could see through the living room windows. Now that he knows, he has not been back, of course. Perhaps he is not a reader. Or maybe he is waiting until after the apocalypse and will return to visit our neighborhood book repository when it is all that is left.

I was in my living room rearranging furniture one day, which is another way of saying that I was putting away books. Our living room is pretty much bookshelves floor to ceiling all around, but they do not hold all of our books, so we have some stacked around on the floor. We put lamps on the stacks and call them end tables but our friends know better. We have a reference section and a poetry section and an anthology section, and from time to time I wonder if we are not ready for a card catalog. While I was working that day, I did a rough count and figured out there are at least fifteen hundred writers living in there, which accounts for how unruly it all seems sometimes. As surprising as it was to me that day, I noticed that I have read an extraordinary number of the books in that room, as well as a fair amount of the ten boxes' worth that I have no shelves for, and the two hundred or so that are in the studio where I write. Including a first printing of the Chartwell Edition of Winston Churchill's *The Second World War*, all four thousand–plus pages of it. It took me a year and a half to read it, working fairly diligently. Even though I am a pacifist, I take Veterans' Day off now every year to reward myself just for having completed it.

But if you ask me what I am reading right now, the answer is really that I am reading one of the same six writers I have been reading almost all of my adult life. I never even go out of town without a copy of something by one of the Six Wise Guys, as I call them. They even have their own separate set of shelves in my studio. These are the only books that I will never lend anyone, but if you want I will read them aloud to you or let you read them, as long as you stay in the yard and promise to put them back when you are finished.

Oh, I am "reading" a lot of other things. I live in a household that puts food on the table and supports its book habit based on what it knows about and who it knows within a certain corner of the literary world. Being a reader seems to be one of the things that goes with being a writer, though to be honest, I cannot say which of the two comes first, or which has been the more powerful in my life.

But what I can say is that what I really am reading is one of those six writers. Or rather, they are reading me. Usually I read two of them at a time. During the course of a year, I read everything that particular one or two has written. If I finish their catalog before the year is up, then I just go back to the beginning and start again. When Christmas comes, I change writers.

Annie Dillard says, "A writer is careful what they read, because what they read is what they will know, and what they know is what they will write." Which is another way to say that the old bromide was wrong— we are not what we eat, we are what we read.

I know for a fact that there is an absolute and

direct relationship between what I read and what I write. I also know that I cannot pray and I cannot be centered and I cannot do the work that has been given me to do whenever what I am reading is not conducive to such.

I got hooked once on a set of murder mysteries. The good news is that I enjoyed them all immensely and I finished the entire set. The bad news is that there are seventeen of them. For months, I was reading stories about murder and deceit, about betrayal and abuse. (It was a little like reading Genesis, now that I think of it.) The whole time, I was wondering why it was that my spirit was so thirsty and my prayer was so dry. I was starving myself and wondering where my strength had gone.

The Six Wise Guys are my teachers and my friends, my mentors and my companions. They write and think in ways that cut me to the core. They lift my spirits with their sense of poetry, make my eyes go blank in wonder at their use of the language. I think I know nearly everything about them and I suspect they know everything about me. I met one of them once and have yet to recover from the experience.

Two of them are dead, the others are still writing. There are three pure novelists, one essayist, and two who write both fiction and nonfiction. They write books about journeys and conversations and dreams and prayers and hopes and fears. They write books about going away and coming home—books about God.

They work and have worked as journalists, writers, poets, clergy, teachers, spies, lawyers, and monks. There are two Catholics, two Anglicans, a Presbyterian, and an Undeclared. Their names for God are different, their writing is not like anyone else's, including each other's, and they tend to avoid the discussion of theology as though it were the plague. Four of them would not admit to having written any theology at all. But they are the best theologians I have ever read.

They have led me, dragged me, tricked me, surprised me, and carried me toward God and myself for years now. If I ever find either one, it will be their fault. They are the ones toward whom and by whom I am drawn in the direction of the Mystery to which I am headed—though drawn and quartered is how they make me feel sometimes. "It is these people, who have come this way," Jean Valentine wrote of her fellow poets, "they are among our veterans, and we need them to look at their lives and at us."

. . .

When I was in the Academy and heard the lectures
about the difference between reading for formation
and reading for information, it seemed to be a sort of
academic curiosity that I could take or leave. In the
mornings, one teacher was working very hard to get
me to use my imagination. And so I was daydreaming
away the hours. In the afternoons, the other was
talking about *lectio* and *meditatio* and *contemplatio,*
and my eyes were just sort of glazing over. They
seemed to be talking about esoteric bits and pieces
of the life of prayer that were behind or beyond me
somehow.

    A friend and I would walk in the afternoons, and I
was carrying around one of the books I was traveling
with at the time. This particular book was one that
was tearing my head off for about the thirteenth time,
and I was reading bits of it aloud to my friend as we
walked. I would read a bit or two, and then we would
walk along in silence for a few minutes, letting it sink
in. I had read some of this stuff to my friend the day
before and I knew I had better let it slowly work its
way into his system or we might have an epiphany
or something close to it break out among us. One

afternoon it occurred to me that *lectio* was not rocket science, I had been doing it for years. And if writers can do it, then anyone can.

Somewhere along the line I had stumbled onto the holy and mysterious ground that is the ground of mental prayer. Perhaps I had just been *fortunatio,* but there it was nonetheless—a step in the Dance of prayer that it seems I have known all along. I simply had not known its name.

"Illumine our minds," we pray, in the words of the prayer that is said to commemorate Saint Alcuin, "that amid the uncertainties and confusion of our own time we may show forth Your eternal truth. . . ." In our more honest moments we know that we do not know the ways of God, that the road to sanctity must lead through wisdom. We sense that our ignorance must be offered up along with the rest of us.

"You caused all holy scriptures to be written for our learning: Grant us to hear them, read, work, learn and inwardly digest them," we pray, "that we may ever hold fast. . . ." We take up the Book of the Story of Us All. We wander its pages, meet its characters, learn its stories. We are breathless at its wisdom, amused by its humor, frightened by its bloodthirstiness, confused by its culture. We find a book that will teach us about the Book, and then another and another. We try our best to make the Story our own, to see ourselves as part of its record. We learn to pray its prayers and recognize its hymns. "Your Word would we hide in our heart," we say, and we mean it, even when we do not understand it, even when it seems dark and without form and void.

"Shed upon us, O LORD, the brightness of Your light." The Word is revealed among us of all places and we seek to be "illumined by the teachings of Your apostles and evangelists," so that we too may walk in the Light. We study the stories of the gospels, trying hard to know what it must have been like to walk by His side. We see ourselves as the blind man and the ones about to throw stones and the tax collector and the fishermen and the cousins in Bethany. We put ourselves in the crowds and we listen to the Sermon and we try to understand what it means to follow. We buy more books and ask more questions, we transpose the stories, and we memorize the lines.

"Enlighten us more and more," we pray, "by the thinking and teaching of scholars. . . ." We know we cannot hope to understand God fully, but each little bit that we learn seems important. We come to trust some guides and to reject others. We look for "what is necessary to be known so that we might love what is to be loved . . . and always to seek to know and follow Your will." We look for saints and for mystics whose words speak to us. We seek out the poets and preachers and pilgrims whose language seems somehow our own, in the hope they will explain what we know we have heard in the depths of our hearts.

"Open our eyes to see," we pray, and our ears to hear and our hearts to feel and our souls to know, "that whatever has any being is a mirror in which we may behold You." Somehow we begin to see God in the stories and songs and tales and poems and paintings and photographs that we did not know God inhabited. We read a favorite novel and suddenly we see the Christ hiding between its lines. We study a treasured photograph and discover His face in the crowd. We listen to a symphony and suspect we hear angels praising the One Who made us.

We begin to acknowledge that the searching has shaped us as much as what we have found. Though we still see through the glass darkly, we find that God reveals Himself more and more.

"We thank You, Almighty God, for this witness," and for that one and for those over there and the ones that are to come, and we pray, "that we may be firmly grounded in its truth."

. . .

To pray in this way—to pray with a book in your hand—is not always as easy as it looks. Not because it is always beyond our ability, but because it is often beyond our willingness.

For one thing, it asks for our time. "Can you not spend one hour with me?" is the question He asks of those who would follow Him, and most of us say that we cannot. "There is the gym, so I can get my high school figure back, and the evening news and some must-see TV and some other stuff that is obviously important. What do you think, I should get up early?"

Such prayer also asks us to trust. It requires that we be willing to trust that the Voice we hear within the lines we read is in fact the Voice that we seek. We have very little confidence in ourselves to hear, and maybe even less confidence that God is actually speaking to anyone these days. The assumption may be that God is speaking only to the professionals about all these things and if there is something we need to know, then they will tell us from the pulpit. "Politics and art are too important to be left to the professionals," said Michelle Shocked. Scripture and sacred writing and prayer are as well.

Most of all, such prayer requires that we abandon

ourselves to it without regard to results. We are taught from the time we hit grade school that energy and efficiency and productivity are more important than anything else. None of those are characteristics or by-products of the prayer that the saints recommend.

And finally it requires that we even let go of our own false sense of control over the Word—the sense that comes to us because we have a good preacher and a set of commentaries and the best new devotional guide from the bestseller list. It is an illusion that must be set aside along with the notion that only "religious" books have anything to say about religion.

If we would dance our way into some deeper communion with God, we must stop working on the Word, wherever it is found, and let it begin to work on us.

Walking in the Dark

You have made us one with Your saints in heaven and earth:
Grant that in our pilgrimage, we may always be supported
by this fellowship of love and prayer,
and know ourselves to be surrounded by their witness
to Your power and mercy.

—From THE PRAYER FOR A SAINT

It has pleased God to make men holy and save them not merely as
individuals . . . by making them into a single people, a people which
acknowledges Him in truth and serves Him in holiness.

—On COMMUNITY

Every vision, every prayer, every meditation is vital
—a kind of critical mass must be achieved.

—EMMA LYTLE

WE DID NOT HIT IT OFF VERY WELL when we first met, or at least if we did I could not tell it. Our first few hours together were pretty miserable, in fact. At least they were for me. I think they were for him as well, though in all the years since, he has never once admitted it.

We were thrown together at the Academy by the luck of the draw, so to speak. We landed in the same covenant group, which meant that for two hours each evening, every night for a week, four times a year for two years, we were to sit in a room with four others besides ourselves and talk about our spiritual journeys and process the day's events and insights and their connection to the life of prayer we were seeking. Right about the thirty-minute mark on the first evening, I was ready to pick up and go home because of his silence and demeanor, and because my inability to dazzle him with my verbal and spiritual footwork had me absolutely intimidated. I was the convener of the group for the first week by virtue of alphabetical order, so I did what any good nervous and slightly overbearing discussion leader would do; I stepped on his toes.

I kept pushing him and pushing him to tell us about himself without any regard for his privacy and his need to go slowly, to take his time with this group of strangers. Finally he let me know I had gone too far. Gently, as is his way, with only twelve or fifteen words, he let me have it.

I was already reasonably certain that I did not belong at the Academy in the first place. Everyone else seemed to be a far piece ahead of me down the road spiritually. When that first covenant session was over, I began to think that since I had already made a fool of myself—usually it takes longer than a day and a half—perhaps I could just quietly pack my things and head for home while everyone was at night prayers and would not notice I was missing until I had a chance to get home and repacked and moved to another state and enrolled in the United Methodist Church Clumsy Convener Protection Program.

According to the rule of the Academy, there was to be silence—the Great Silence, it was called—in all of the buildings from the end of night prayers until morning prayers at seven o'clock the next day. If you wanted to talk, you had to go outside and away from the buildings. A fair number of us adopted the Sumatanga Corollary to the Rule: the practice of the Great Walkabout before the Great Silence. We would walk along the road that led to and through the camp and hope for a Great Conversation before bedtime.

On the third or fourth night, as night prayers were finishing up and people were heading off in the silent manner we were beginning to adopt, he gave me the Sumatanga version of Trappist sign language for "Do you want to walk tonight and if so meet me at the front porch in ten minutes." In a little while the two of us were walking down that two-lane road in the countryside of northern Alabama in the dark, so dark that I could hardly see anything at all. We walked for almost an hour before either one of us ever said anything, right down the middle of the road, moving to the shoulder once or twice when a car came along.

I do not usually get very excited about walking in the dark. I cannot see well in the night, and noises in the woods make me jumpy even in broad daylight. I found out later that he had spent two years walking point in Vietnam, so the dark we were walking through was not scary to him at all. The first thing

I learned from him was this: If you are going to walk in the dark, walk with someone who can see in the dark.

Much of the life of prayer is lived alone. Much of it can only be practiced that way. Going into your closet to pray is by definition a rather solitary exercise. It can be lonely.

Silence, confession, journaling, contemplation, meditation, retreat—many of the things that one does in search of the Silence itself are done alone, even if, as in the case a monastic setting or a place like the Academy, they are done in community. The witness of the saints, and some of us not so saintly types, is that even in the most congenial and compatible of communities, the one who seeks to live a life of prayer is very often, most often, alone. The paradox is that such a life cannot be lived by yourself. It is not, ultimately, even for yourself.

One of the great risks of any serious attempt to live a life of prayer is that it can easily become insular and self-centered. That it can become a search for some idyllic place where it is just "God and me," where no one interferes, where no one's problems and needs and wants get in the way of one's being holy and devout and prayerful and saintly.

Another risk is that the journey inward never makes its final turn, the turn to becoming the journey outward. To pray only for oneself is about as meaningful a practice as saying the liturgy only for oneself. The liturgy is not for me, it is for God. Ultimately, my prayer is not for me, it is for those who have been given to me and to whom I have been given.

But it is still so solitary in so many ways that one can get lost out there in the dark fairly easily without another set of eyes to help one see from time to time. The way that one might get lost in the woods in Alabama, for instance.

I went to a weekend retreat in which thirty or so of us had gathered to spend a couple of days working in small groups to explore questions about spirituality and vocation and such. At the close of the retreat, the leader began to say a closing prayer while the group stood in a circle. It had been a rich time for all of us, and we held hands as we stood together and he began to pray. As he did so, one began to get a sense of the transcendent as he lifted the group in prayer. He spoke of our collective dreams and fears and hopes, and of our deep desire to be a part of the building of the kingdom. For a few moments, or so it seemed, we were lifted together in prayer in some deep way that I had not known before.

Afterward, as the group began to scatter through the room, saying their goodbyes, gathering up coats and bags and scarfing up the last few cookies on the snack table, I heard a friend say to the man who had prayed for us all, "That must have been draining, that prayer."

"Yes," he said, "I suppose that it was."

What he had done, I think, was to lay down his life in a way that is as deeply important as any that we have to offer each other. If we pray, and if we believe that God listens to our prayer, then to spend that audience on behalf of someone else is an act of selflessness that is larger than it seems. At some level, our prayer—spoken or unspoken, written or read aloud, experienced in silence or lived out in the work of our hands and feet—is all that we have to offer each other. And it can be the best that we ever give each other as well.

. . .

There must be something to the Church's insistence on the whole notion of praying for each other, if for no other reason than that there is no other reason for it.

The cynic in me (or the skeptic, he said, giving himself the benefit of the doubt) can easily understand the Church's encouraging us to tithe, to show up on Sunday, and to bring our children to Sunday school. Some sense of marketing alone explains all of that, even if there were no spiritual value to any of it, which there clearly is. One cannot maintain the Church militant without supplies and resources, without regular attendance, or without a steady stream of new recruits. But one could not maintain the Kiwanis Club either without the same sort of things.

But why pray for each other? Because Jesus said so? Jesus also said to go barefoot and give your cloak away to people who steal your shirt and let the dead bury the dead, and we have managed to get ourselves off the hook for those things. But to pray for each other? To spend my audience with God on someone who may well not deserve it or appreciate it or may well even have an audience of their own?

And how to pray for someone else? For a fair

amount of the time, we are not even sure what to pray for, even if we were certain that God listens, and at times it is hard to be certain even of that, considering that very often it seems that the things we pray for most are the very things to which God pays attention the least.

Some of us have a hard time asking for things when we pray, even for ourselves, perhaps especially for ourselves. To ask for certain blessings or acts of grace when God knows what we need better than we do seems pretentious. To recount to God our own prospective solutions for family or friends or world peace or what to do about global warming seems superfluous as well. If we can trust God with our own life, then we can trust God with the lives of those we love and care for, and the planet we live on for that matter. To be sure, the most important things that ever happened to me were all surprises anyway, rather than things for which I prayed.

Perhaps God does not need me to pray for myself or for others because He needs help figuring out what to do or needs some degree of persuasion on our part before He is willing to do good for somebody. Perhaps God needs me to pray so that I can be about the business of laying myself and the people and places and things I care about on the altar. It is okay if I do not know what is to happen next. I just need to be laying them out on the rocks—with hope, with faith, with diligence, with attention, with compassion.

Then I need to listen, listen for the prayer of God that is rising in my heart, perhaps for the prayer that I should be praying rather than the one that I am praying.

When Keenan died, we got a call from one of our friends to tell us the news. We were surprised, because we had not even known this was the day that Keenan was to arrive, much less the day that he was to leave. Keenan had been alive when he started through the birth canal, but he was gone by the time he was delivered.

The hospital is near our house, so I decided that I would go over to be with Gary and Mary Lou, the parents who had waited for Keenan to arrive and now had to let him go. I had no earthly idea what to say to them, but I wanted to be there.

If there are people on earth who know and dislike Gary and Mary Lou, I cannot imagine who they are or why they feel that way. The only possible flaw I can think of is that some people are jealous of the fact that Gary and Mary Lou make the prettiest children in the world. They have four, Keenan was the fifth, and some of us suspect that they keep having them just to show off the caliber of their gene pool. It would be somewhat easier to live with if their children were obnoxious or spoiled or bratty, but they are not, not one of them.

It is not hard to imagine what it was like in the birthing room that morning some two hours or so after what was to be such a joyous day had turned into something else altogether. Nothing that anyone did or said, or even could do or say, changed that or ever will. It was just sad and heartbreaking, and it still is, and it always will be.

As the news spread around town, people began to do the only thing they could: they began to pray. Many of them did so with their hands.

One came and sat with Mary Lou while she held Keenan and said goodbye to the sweet boy she had never really had a chance to say hello to. Another came to be on the telephone in the waiting room and make the calls that spread the word. At another telephone, another friend was beginning the process of making the arrangements, the process we have all seen and dread to think about having to do.

Someone else came to stay with the older children

until Gary could get home with the terrible news instead of with a new baby brother. Someone else sat with Mary Lou while she waited for Gary to return.

Somebody called the grandparents and somebody called the church folks and somebody called the business associates. Somebody went to the grocery and somebody took the kids to the park so that Gary could get some rest and cry some tears.

Together, they "prayed" the prayer of intercession, the prayer of shouldering the burdens of others.

"Take up your cross and follow me," said the Teacher to His friends. And as long as you are down there in the dust, help someone lift their cross too.

Somewhere along the road in Sumatanga, one night in the dark, my Academy friend and I suddenly discovered that we were walking along talking about our encounter with the Christ, barely able to contain ourselves as we questioned and connected and exclaimed and wondered aloud. We had begun to tell our stories and jump from one idea to the next. "This is what it must have been like to be one of the disciples," we agreed. We would walk a few yards and then stop and start talking excitedly, putting the various threads of our lives into some sort of pattern that had begun to make itself known for the first time.

We walked for six hours that night. Our hearts, as did those of the two disciples along the road to Emmaus, fairly "burned within us." Neither one of us remembers exactly what was said, except that we said everything there was to say to each other about everything we held dear. Before the night was over, we made a promise to each other: that we would travel together from now on, that we would pray for each other each day, that we would help to shoulder each other's burdens when we could, that we would intercede on each other's behalf.

In the years that have passed since that night, his prayer for me has taken many forms. He drove from his home in Illinois on Easter weekend as soon as he heard that I was in the hospital. He stayed in my town all weekend even though the doctors would only allow us to see each other for thirty minutes each day.

When I began to write seriously, after all the years of talking about it rather than actually doing it, he called me once a week, at the same time on the same day of the week, to "ask" me if I would mind reading what I had written the week before. He knew that I needed both the encouragement and the accountability to help me until my own confidence and discipline were strong enough to send me to the studio to work every day the way I am called to do.

He came to town to be the best man at my wedding, and by most accounts, he was certainly that. He talks to my kids on the telephone when he happens to call when they happen to be here. He lent me money once when I was in dire straits and would not take it back even if I had it. He flew into town once for a birthday party in our backyard, and another time when we had some good news at our house and decided that we had better celebrate.

The list goes on and on. Telephone call after telephone call, note after note, visit after visit, retreat after retreat. He will tell you that I have even been nice to him a time or two as well.

"What a good friend he is to you," people say to me sometimes. And it is true.

But we are not friends because we work together or went to school together or attend the same church or live in the same neighborhood. We do not even have very much in common. If we did work together or live down the street from each other, it is not too terribly likely that we would be friends at all—if for no other reason than that we are both so shy we might never have said hello to each other.

What binds us together is the prayer, the promise and the lifting of each other's burdens, the commitment we have made, and kept, to be companions to each other on the road that we share. What binds us together is the laying down of our lives for each other in a way that we cannot even explain.

I was once a part of a non–Sunday school Sunday school class. Four or five of us started it when we discovered our common interest in prayer after months of bumping into each other in the little prayer chapel during the church school hour. We discovered that we also had a common disinterest in the kind of discussion that is to be found in many adult classes on Sunday mornings, the kind where everyone enthusiastically discusses stuff that nobody is ever going to know anyway, like whether or not Jesus was popular in high school during the "lost years," or whether Paul went blind or was in some sort of trance induced by religious ecstasy, and does it have anything to do with snake handlers in east Tennessee, or what Jesus would think if He came back to earth and visited our church and stuck around for the service after He had turned the tables on us.

Although the director of program at our church

was not very enthusiastic about it, we managed to wangle a classroom and a spot on the official adult class listing and began to meet on Sunday mornings to pray together, or at least to talk about prayer. We had a name for the class and a class roll that sometimes people actually filled out and returned to the church office. We had a lectern too, just in case anyone ever felt like they knew enough to try to teach the class, but as near as I can remember, it stayed over in the corner and collected dust, because that never happened.

The class rules were pretty simple. You had to be willing to buy and use the prayer book that we had agreed together to use in some way in our daily lives. You had to pray each day in some sort of regular and disciplined way and report that out to someone in the group each week. Finally, you had to be willing to share whatever light you happened to stumble into with the rest of us when we gathered on Sunday mornings. These rules seemed like enough, so we did not have any more.

One day the discussion rolled around to intercessory prayer. I recall that it was occasioned by one of our number being in some circumstance that clearly called for us to pray for him, and we clearly felt a responsibility to do so. It was just that at a certain level we did not quite know how to do it.

I am not sure that any of us ever quite knows how to pray when it is time to pray for others. Do you ask God to remove the pain and suffering even though you know in your heart that such things are the stuff of life itself, and particularly the stuff of the spiritual life, the stuff that makes us more like Christ than anything else? Do you try to figure out what is right, at least by your own lights, and explain it to God over and over until He finally catches on and fixes it up properly? Do you spend a lot of time explaining to God all of the things you say you believe God already knows? It can be a little intimidating to give direction to the LORD of the Universe. It makes many of us nervous. The ones who are not should be.

Yet there it is in front of us, the call to pray for each other. There is Jesus praying for His disciples on the night of their last big dinner party together, unless you want to count the cookout by the lake. There is Paul reminding community after community in his letters, "Do not forget to pray for each other." There is the cry of our hearts that tells us that if we have any influence at all with the Father, now is the time to spend it, when one we love and care for is in need.

So on this day when we were all struggling with the issue, Charles explained it to us. He did not mean to exactly, but explain it he did.

Charles is a university professor and he looks the part. He is a big man, with a kind of bewildered-by-the-culture look about him, and the sort of clothes that one expects from a professor. He was always one of my favorite people in the class. He and I had in common, among other things, a sense that we would have both been happy to be born a century earlier, except for college basketball and indoor plumbing and being able to talk to our children long-distance.

We are both card-carrying members of the group that Huston Smith calls "wounded Christians—those for whom the church has not lived up to its own rhetoric and has left them empty and lost." Yet we had both returned to the Church, and gladly too. Our time away had meant a lot to us, though a lot of it was really hard, and we had returned certain somehow that we would find there the things that we sought.

I remember Charles saying, on that Sunday, that he hardly knew how to pray for himself, much less anyone else. "So I just say their names," he said, "and sort of picture them in the last place I saw them. Then I am quiet for as long as I can be, just sort of lifting them up in my mind, looking at their face, trying to see what it holds. And for a while it seems that I am carrying a part of whatever they are having to carry."

To the Father, on that last night with His friends, Jesus said, "I lift up to You those You have given me." To lift up those who have been given to us, and to whom we have been given, is all, and possibly everything, that we can do.

"Father Almighty," we pray, "we offer prayers to You for those whose lives are linked to ours." And there they are, in those places where they were the last time we saw them. We can see the way their hair curls around their ears just so, and the twinkle in their eyes, and the hint of something unnamed that hides in the edges and folds of their smiles. We have been given to them, and they to us, by virtue of blood and gene pool or by virtue of relationship and covenant. We are not alone, and neither are they, no matter how lonely we seem, all of us and any of us, at times.

They are our friends and brothers and sisters and daughters and sons and loved ones. They are our enemies sometimes too, those with whom we are in conflict. "Pray even for those who curse you," the

Teacher said, and I expect that would apply as well to those who simply annoy you and to those who bug the living daylights out of you. But it is hard to truly hate those for whom you truly pray. Those with whom you have a hard time have been given to you just as surely as those with whom you are at peace.

"We pray to You for our companions in the Way, those to whom we have promised our faithfulness, prayers, and companionship. . . ." The circle widens to include those whose lives are linked to ours by the communities of which we are a part, large and small, formal and informal. Those to whom we have said: "I'll pray for you." "If we can do anything at all, call us." "You are not alone, remember, I will be with you." "I will be thinking about you that day."

You can see them in your mind's eye this day, off to see the doctor who may have bad news or headed down the road to a new town. They will go in and out of courtrooms and classrooms and birthing rooms this day. They will come home, they will go away, they will return, they will leave you behind, they will leave forever. If you could be beside them, you would; if you can pray for them, you must.

"We pray for the holy catholic Church, and for all who seek the truth . . . and for those who faithfully serve Your household as true servants and stewards of Your Divine Mysteries . . . for those we have known who have taught us Your Story and shown us Your ways. . . ." We pray for the bishop with whom we do not agree all the time, and the new pastor whose ways we are learning. For the little church we visited on vacation, the one where the little man seemed so glad to see us and whose face fell when we told him we were only passing through, and for the couple there who invited you home for lunch even though their hearts were trembling with fear because one of them had just learned she had a brain tumor.

We pray for those who have welcomed us to the Table and for the Sunday school teacher who taught us who David and Goliath and Moses and all the rest were, and for the pastor who put his arms around you when you were twelve and more afraid and yet more certain that you had met Jesus than you have ever been again.

"We lift to You those in whom we have seen the face of the Christ this day. . . ." The little girl selling magazines door-to-door, the schoolteacher who spends her days caring for children who will someday only remember her smile and not her name. The drunk on the corner, and the one in your living room, both of them afraid and alone and awash in some fear and pain they cannot name. The broken ones and the young ones, the afflicted and the lost, the forgotten and the astonished, who brought us some glimpse of the hungry and naked and imprisoned Christ, naked in their joy and grief and hope and pain and wonder and toil.

"We entrust all who are dear to us to Your never-failing love and care, for this life and the life to come, knowing that You will do for them far more than we can desire or pray for."

Anne Sexton, the poet, had a notion that there was a single poem, "a communal poem, being written by all of the poets alive." We poets like to think of such a thing. Most of us believe it too, I think, or at least we should. Those of us who pray might do well to think something similar about our prayer.

What else can we do? Can we heal those for whom we pray, can we always hold them, can we even know what some of them might need this day?

Of this one thing can we be certain: They have been given to us and we to them, and we have promised to share their journey and their burdens.

We have promised to lay down our very lives for them, even on the days when the road they travel is so far away from us that we would not know where to throw ourselves down if we could muster the courage to do so. So we lift them up, sharing some bit of the burden and hoping and praying that someone else is shouldering a bit of it too, so that the burdens can be lifted, or failing that, at least carried somehow by us all, if we will carry them together the way we have been called to do.

"*Kyrie, eleison; Christe, eleison.* LORD, have mercy; Christ, have mercy," we pray, we simply pray. For we must, we simply must. It is all that we who walk together in the dark can do.

Signs and Wonders

Make this a temple of Your presence and a place of prayer.
Be always near us when we seek You in this place.

—From THE PRAYERS FOR
CONSECRATING A CHURCH

An action performed or an object observed,
which has special religious significance, is called a sign . . .
they instill a spiritual response on
the part of the one observing the object or observing the action.

—On SIGNS

The beginning of wisdom is to get yourself a roof.

—AFRICAN PROVERB

ACTUALLY I ALREADY HAD A ROOF, so I got a rug instead. I was not certain that acquiring the rug would actually bring me wisdom any more than having a roof had done. I have to admit that I got it because of the Morgan Freeman character in a film version of *Robin Hood.* Freeman played the part of Azeem, a Muslim who had come west with Robin after Robin saved his life in a prison escape in the Middle East during the Crusades. Azeem had sworn to return the favor and so he followed Robin to England.

There is a funny scene at the beginning of the film in which Azeem spends a fair amount of time grumbling at the difficulties of telling the time of day by the mostly absent sun in the gray skies over England. "No wonder you English are heathens, you cannot tell when it is time to pray. You cannot even find the east," he says, and finally unfolds his prayer rug and falls to his knees to say his prayers. Robin is, of course, attacked by the evil sheriff's men while the man who had sworn to protect him is saying his prayers. The oath regarding prayers evidently took precedence over an oath sworn to protect English infidels. While Azeem offers thanksgivings and blessings to Allah, Robin shouts for Azeem to hurry up and finish because he himself is not yet ready to meet his Maker.

I have read or seen nearly all the versions of the Robin Hood story and I do not recall the Moor ever appearing before. I expect the filmmakers introduced him in an attempt to drive a certain demographic segment of the potential moviegoing public into the theaters. What it drove me to was my knees. Why don't we Christians have rugs? I wondered.

Maybe they could be handed out with each profession of faith. Maybe we could carry them in a quiver, as did the Moor. Maybe we could fit them into the newspaper pouch on our briefcases or the front pocket of our gym bags.

In the Islamic tradition, prayers are said by the devout at five different times each day. In the cities and towns of the Middle East, the horn is sounded in the mosques, and the faithful stop what they are doing and face the east to pray. Traffic stops, stores close, commerce ceases. They say the ancient prayers of their tradition, the liturgies and thanksgivings and blessings, the prayers that are suited to the time of the day and the season of the year.

Those who live too far away to hear the trumpet sound note the time and kneel to pray. Those who can go to the mosque itself for prayers. Those who cannot be present in the mosque, cannot make their way to the holy place that has been reserved for prayer and for worship of the Almighty, use a rug to bring the sanctuary to them. The uninitiated observer may think that these people are kneeling on a rug to keep their knees clean; the ones doing the kneeling think they are in the presence of God.

"So you want to meet God," said a priest to me once. "And just where will this meeting take place?"

The rug that I use now for prayers was given to me by someone I love. It was originally a gift for me to use for picnics and such with my children, which I have done. It was made in India and is striped with all sorts of bright colors that seem more suited to picnics than to prayer, I guess, and it was never blessed by a priest or anything official at all. It bears the stains of mustard and potato salad, and I am pretty certain that is a Chianti stain in the left-hand corner. The cleaning instructions said that you were not supposed to wash the rug, but dry cleaning always seemed a little much for a picnic rug, and so I have never done much more than sweep it or hang it on a fence and slap the dust out of it. Someday I will have to have it cleaned, I suppose, if it does not fall apart first. It is a pretty tough rug, though. One of my relatives has one just like it in her carport and she parks her Toyota on it, for some reason that I do not understand and have always been afraid to ask.

After I saw the Moor in the film, I started using the rug as a place to say my prayers. There were no more instructions for that than there were for having a picnic on it, but I discovered that it is not too complicated; even Protestants can do it.

I have come to believe that one of the steps in the Dance is about place. In every tradition one can find the stories of the search for God's place, for the sacred space in which the presence of God can be sought and found. Places that have been set aside for God to inhabit, places that have been marked for worship and prayer, places to which those who are seeking God have been called forth to hope and rest and listen.

Such places do not fall into the category of one size fits all. They range from adobe buildings built by Indians at the direction of missionaries in the American Southwest to the great cathedrals in the old cities of Europe. From spectacular mosques and temples in the East to simple white frame buildings dotting the landscapes of the farm fields in the Delta and the Dakotas. They have pews and chairs and hardwood floors, or they have bricks and stones and kneelers. They house great pipe organs and choirs and cantors and readers, or they have pianos and guitars and song leaders and special singers. They are filled with the sound of plainsong and bells, or gospel tunes and tambourines, or the a cappella voices of children singing a Wesley tune. We go to such places on the Sabbath, whichever day of the week that is for us, because we want to worship and we want, at least for a moment, to be still and know that He is God.

Where to find God the rest of the time is the question. Where do we find a sacred space in between our Sabbath journeys over the river and through the woods to God's house? Does God simply lie low in between Sabbaths, hiding out in some corner of the sanctuary until we return?

We can go to church every time the doors are open and still have great huge gaps in time when there is no sanctuary for us, no place to bow our heads and worship, no place to kneel and pray and offer praise and thanksgiving. Does that mean we need to make such a place closer to home? Azeem suggested to me that I get a rug and keep it handy, right along with the other things I need to make my way through the life we live here.

One morning very early I sort of crept into the living room to say my prayers. It was rug day, the first day I was going to use it as a place of prayer. I unfolded it a little sheepishly. No one but me is ever awake that time of day at my house, and I barely am myself sometimes, but I was still nervous about being found doing something that was so far from the tradition in which I grew up. "I saw it in *Robin Hood*" did not seem like a defense that would stand much theological scrutiny in the circles I have traveled in so far.

The rug and I sort of stared at each other for a while, and then I sat down on it. It took almost a week of staring it down every morning before I found myself able to actually kneel on it, self-consciously at first but nonetheless closer to prostrate before the LORD than I had ever been.

We middle-class Western Protestants are not very big on what some might call the trappings of religion, the sorts of things that are symbolic, the sorts of things that might call attention to ourselves. We tend to be suspicious and a bit condescending of rosaries and yarmulkes and the like. Oh, you see a "God Is My Copilot" bumper sticker from time to time—you can even buy them at the checkout when you get your car washed at the corner in the town where I live—but that seems different somehow. A fair number of the people who have those stickers cannot drive very well at all in my estimation, leading me to wonder if we would not all be safer if they went ahead and turned the wheel over to the copilot. I have never seen any of those drivers pull over and drop to their knees to say their prayers. They never seem to miss the rush hour or the evening news, but I think it unlikely they are rushing to get to Vespers.

As a group we sort of regard such religious trappings as being somehow superstitious or idolatrous or comic. It seems to me that we should be careful not to thumb our noses at those who pause to light candles in a two-hundred-year-old church as they make prayers of intercession to the saints on behalf of those they love.

You will not find any shrines in our houses the way you do in Mexico City, or mezuzahs on the doorframes the way you do in Bethlehem, or prayer rugs beside the book bags the way you do in Mecca. Most days you could walk in and out of hundreds of houses in my neighborhood and have no clue at all as to whether the people who live there are religious people or not. And I expect that some of them are. I do live, as singer/songwriter Marcus Hummon points out, "right here on the buckle of the Bible Belt."

Our spiritual forebears set many such things aside as a way to make a statement about the excesses of the Church in their time. They were right to do so, I expect. At least, I have read about it some and understand it, I think, and I know how and why we ended up without some of those ancient habits and practices. But I have also noticed that we no longer go in for the modest dress that they recommended as an alternative to expensive clothes. Nor do we take the Eucharist as regularly, or give alms to the poor without making sure they use them wisely, or sing songs on street corners much these days.

Our forebears' fear of ostentation has pretty much faded from our memories. Our shirts say Polo, our shoes say Nike, our cars say Lexus, and our luggage says Hartman. Our lawns say we are successful, our houses say we are well off, our church buildings say we are pretty fair fund-raisers.

But I think our lives are saying that we need some sacred spaces and sacred things in them. We need some things that are as mysterious as the Mystery itself. What might happen to us and among us if we regained the sense of mystery that we have replaced with a list of answers and formulas and glib slogans that are of little help in the face of the troubling questions of our day? What might become of us if we had a corner in our houses where the only thing that was done there was prayer—a place apart, a place set aside for God to inhabit or at least visit during the times between the Sabbaths, when we are invited to God's own house to visit? What might happen if we found ourselves daily in such a sacred space, on our knees in worship? Or simply sitting there in a chair?

We would not have to go so far as to light candles or have kneeling benches or icons or anything, though it might not hurt. We would not even have to stop traffic or take the telephone off the hook. It would not require that we forgo yet another handsome newsreader's reading of the news that is the same news we heard in the car on the way home from work, news that has likely not changed much since we got it from the local anchorwoman this morning over breakfast.

It would be okay if such sacred places and observances made us self-conscious at first, or even forever. If it got too bad we could go into our closet and pray, as was suggested to us some time ago by the One in Whose name we pray, a suggestion that has fallen by the wayside as we stuffed more stuff into our closets.

Every writer I know writes in a different place and in a different way from every other writer I know. But they all have a place to write. A place that has been set apart for it. They do it because they know that to live the life of an artist, you must produce art. Otherwise, you are just cleverly avoiding the curse of the dreaded day job and maintaining an excuse to be shy and wear funny clothes. Having a place helps to produce art, if for no other reason than that at least you have a place to go and hope such a mysterious thing will take place. To live a life of prayer, one must produce prayer.

Which is harder to do if you have no place in which to do so. "We can talk to God anywhere," we say, and it is true. But more often than not, because we do not have a somewhere to talk to God, we talk to God nowhere. One can build an altar in one's heart, of course, but it can take some time, according to the saints. Most of us could use the reminder that might come to us if we would put an altar in our house while we pray for the day in which we ourselves become the living sacrifice such an altar deserves.

Any place can be made more or less sacred, depending on what we ourselves bring to it. Our own attitudes and expectations and actions can contribute or not to the sacredness of the place. A temple can become a den of thieves, or so I have heard. A picnic rug can become a sanctuary, or so I have found.

"We thank You for the faith that we have inherited, in all of its rich variety. It sustains our life. . . ." Perhaps more than we know. How many prayers said by the faithful on our behalf has it taken to bring us in safety to this very day in this very place? There was the schoolteacher who unbeknownst to anyone said our name in her living room every morning, and the uncle who prayed over the family photos on the mantel. And long before them, perhaps an ancestor who prayed the rosary or was the one who was the first in his family to be baptized. And there must have been a long line of pilgrims and saints who attended the masses and took the sacraments and meditated on the icons and copied the scriptures so that we, whose life and times they could never have imagined, might become a part of the Body of Christ.

"And now we thank You for this place where we may be still and know that You are God. . . ." It is a room or a corner or a seat in the window. It is on the back porch or the front one, it is in the garden or out back by the tree. It is the place at your place where you go to pray, to say your office, to read the scripture, to, as Mary did, "ponder these things in your heart."

It may well be a place that does double duty and becomes sanctuary only when you are there to offer your prayers. It is a "closet" to go into to pray that is in plain sight, only you know that it becomes a sanctuary at times. At other times it remains a living room or a corner or the table in the backyard, and no one but you knows its hidden and sacred meaning.

But it is sanctuary to you for those moments

when you go there to meet God, to offer praise and petition and the prayer of your heart.

"Grant that in these earthly things we may behold the order and beauty of things heavenly. . . ." go the words of the old prayer. These earthly things—the icons and the candles, the books and the cross, the tokens and the mementos that remind you to pray.

It is the rosary you hold that the nuns gave to your father as he lay dying. It is the smooth stone you brought home from your first retreat. It is that necklace you have worn since your confirmation, it is the mark you make beside your name. It is the rug you sit on to pray and the cross on the wall by the door, the cross you touch each time you leave home.

They are the things, the earthly things, that remind you to pay attention for the Voice and to trust that it will speak to you. They are the things of this world that remind you of the world beyond.

"May it be that here we are made one with You and with one another, so that our lives are sustained and sanctified for Your service. . . ." When you come to this place, you are not alone. As you say your prayers and make your meditations, your solitude and prayer is joined to that of others, to the community of saints past and saints present and saints to come.

You are joined by the monks of Gethsemani and by the abbas and ammas of the desert. Your morning office is offered alongside that of the faithful all over the world and all over your town. At the moment that you say the Our Father, some of your brothers and sisters are saying it as well. You know some of their names, but most of them are unknown to you and always will be. But you are one with them nonetheless, for this moment at least.

My rug and I have been a lot of places together. I still have sand in it from this year's trip to the beach. It still doubles as a picnic rug; the people with whom I picnic will not let me retire it. It is somehow all right to me to break bread with the ones I love the most on the rug where I listen for the voice of the One Who loves me best.

I take it with me when I go on retreat with the friends with whom I have been praying and walking and wondering and struggling along the Road for the last few years. We often spread it out on the table that holds the bread and wine and candles and cross that we gather around each day to break bread and remember why and how we are friends in the first place and where this journey has been and is leading. It seems okay that as you unfold it, there is sand from your children's sand castles and wine spills from the days when you were courting your wife and grass stains from listening to Bach in the park mingled in with the bread crumbs and the candle wax and the imprints of the cross in this sacred space where we are about to share the meal that matters the most.

I took it to the hospital once when I was ill. I took it because it was like a friend to me, and where I was going I was not sure I was returning from, and wherever that turned out to be, I did not want to be without it. Each morning (earlier and earlier as I got used to the fact that doctors make their rounds before their patients are awake, perhaps just to be perverse), I would spread the rug out and sit in the light from the rising sun. Most days I did not pray any words at all, unless weeping out of fear and despair counts as a language to be understood by someone. I have a friend who said to me once that "in prayer, all sorrow is allowed," and most all of mine was there with me in those days.

My psychiatrist came in one morning while I was sitting there. I looked up, startled, and he looked down, embarrassed, and then he stepped back into the hallway the way he would have had he come upon me naked. Which is what happened, in a way. I was not strong enough to dance before the LORD, but I did manage to get dressed.

I was a little nervous about what he might say about my rug when he came into the room after I called out that it was okay to come in. It is hard for a forty-year-old to explain to his psychiatrist that he needs his rug as much as his daughter used to need her blankie.

"Everyone needs a place," was all he said.

Which is, of course, wisdom, or at least the beginning of it.

Dancing on the Head of a Pen

Give us grace, we pray,
joyfully to do the things You have given us to do
knowing that nothing is menial or common
that is done for Your sake.

—From THE PROPER
for FEBRUARY 27

An examination of conscience made daily or at special intervals
as a devotional practice . . . enables one to eliminate faults and
imperfections . . . and helps to develop the opposing virtues.

—On EXAMEN

Pursue, keep up with, circle round and round your life. . . . Know your
own bone: gnaw at it, bury it, unearth it, and gnaw at it still.

—HENRY DAVID THOREAU

IN THE STUDIO WHERE I WRITE, there are two sets of things that I pull out from time to time to read through so that I have a better sense of who and where I am.

One of them is a folder full of letters and notes and cards from people who have said kind things about me and my work. It is the writer's equivalent of one of those "bragging books" that grandmothers carry to show off pictures of their grandchildren.

Sometimes, I find myself in a place where I cannot even begin to imagine that anyone would ever want to read anything that I am writing. Sometimes it helps to be able to pull out the folder and read some of the letters to myself. It doesn't take too long to go through them; there are not many of them, and I have already memorized the best parts. When I read them, it makes me feel good enough about what I am trying to do to actually try to do some more of it. So far, I have not found it necessary to carry my bragging book around with me in my purse, but I am probably not above it if the going gets too tough.

The other things I read through every now and then are my old journals, or rather some of them—there are quite a few. I can pretty much count on any one or two of them to reduce the swelling of my ego pretty quickly.

Writing in a journal is a funny thing to do in some ways. For one thing, who am I talking to?

Sometimes, especially if you are one who writes books, you imagine that it is for someone to find years from now, to read and to be astonished at your insight and devotion and courage and grace in the face of struggle and pain. They will, of course, recognize it for the great literary treasure it is, and it will be published to enormous critical acclaim and tremendous popular success and will come to be considered one of the great works of twentieth-century literature.

In my more lucid moments, I have come to suspect that will not be what happens with my journals, though sometimes I find myself "editing" as I go, just in case.

No matter how tempting it is to think that what I put on the page every day might be great literary stuff or profound and sacred truth, the actual truth is very different. Most days it is very ordinary—painfully so, in fact—very often the same ordinary stuff that I wrote about the day before. The same miserable bit of business can be on the top of my head and the tip of my pen for days and weeks at a time, like a bad pop song that rings in my head and will not go away.

Sometimes, the pages of a journal can become a place to think out loud—to rant and rave and release one's hurt and anger and fear and frustration without exploding all over someone. It can be a place to wonder out loud at the possibilities and ramifications of a particular circumstance or decision or event or encounter. From time to time one can discover and see and touch one's own feelings and hopes and dreams and joys. Sometimes one can practice conversations that are bound to take place or write letters that must never be posted.

Sometimes it seems that I write in it only because I like my own company and the sound of my own voice. A measure of which is probably good, two measures of which are probably not.

I have written in journals most all my life. The first one I have is dated when I was thirteen. I have at various times thought of journaling as literature, as practice for my craft, as history, as memoir. The habit has been friend and foe to me, comfort and obsession, exhilarating and painful.

Until recently, I never thought of it as holy.

. . .

I have two friends with whom I go on retreat two or three times a year. We have been doing that for several years now. When we are together, one of the things that we do is decide what time we will meet for morning prayers to begin our day. The time we set then determines what time we will get up to exercise before morning prayers. They get up and walk a couple of miles, I get up and drink a couple of pots of coffee.

I am always a little embarrassed when they come back from their walk. They are wide awake and grinning, looking healthier than they did the day before. I am sitting cross-legged on a bench, coffee at my side, my journal in my lap, looking as tormented as I did yesterday.

One day one of them said to me, "Why do you get up so early just to do that? You cannot possibly like coffee that much."

"Oh," I replied in the most literary manner I could muster up so early in the day, "I am journaling."

"Perhaps it is prayer," the other said.

"No, no, no," I said, "nothing so sacred or profound as that."

"Perhaps it is the deepest prayer that a writer can pray," he said, and went off to shower.

. . .

At first, I resisted the notion of my journal as the deep prayer of a writer because I know better than anyone else just how shallow my journal can be. To dignify it with the claim that it is prayer seemed presumptuous and pretentious, to say the least.

Then I went through a stretch in which I had trouble with the notion that something that came so naturally, so easily to me could be considered prayer. There was no sacrifice to it, how could it be holy? All I seemed to be missing was a two-mile power walk or *Good Morning America,* neither of which was very appealing to me.

"Let your prayer rise from within you," says Ed Farrell.

The holiness of this act, the holiness that makes it prayer for me, is to be found in the fact that it does rise naturally from me, that it always draws me to it, that it has been a constant companion to me for as long as I can remember.

"The page, the page, will teach you to write," says Annie Dillard. The page, the page has taught me to pray.

Much of the life of prayer seems to me to be

about learning to pay attention. One finds and adapts and adopts the traditions of prayer that can be added to the fabric of one's life. They, in turn, lead to acts of devotion and oblation and sacrifice in the hope that one's heart will be increasingly prepared to be present to and shaped by the ways of God.

To pray the offices or to follow the calendar or to pray the Psalter or to pray the scriptures is to commit oneself to the act of coming to attention at particular times and in particular ways. It is to provide a frame upon which one's life can be lived and within which one's journey can be made. The discipline of such prayer is necessary in greater or lesser degree for different people. And the fruits of such prayer will vary from person to person, and even from time to time within the life of one person. To offer yourself up to such habits and traditions and disciplines is to allow yourself to be shaped by the prayer traditions that have been given to us by those who have learned the Dance before us. It is to trust that the habits of the heart that shaped the saints are powerful enough to shape us as well.

But there is more to the life of prayer. For we must discover the prayer of our own heart. And that prayer, the prayer of God that rises up within us, the prayer of our heart that is known only to God and can be discovered only by us—that prayer is buried in the story of our own lives. It is a story that is likely to go untold, even to ourselves, unless we are willing to let a page teach us to pray.

I have kept a journal for long enough to know all of the reasons why people claim they cannot keep them. In fact, I can talk myself out of doing it a lot faster than I can talk anyone into doing it.

I know that it takes too much time and that we do not have any to spare. I know that most days what will be written down will not be very artful or sacred, that it is unlikely that we will ever write anything so profound that we will be moved to tears by the sheer power of our own words.

I am well aware that most of us do not consider ourselves creative enough or particularly literate enough to feel we might write anything down that is worth anyone ever reading. Which is fine, since no one is going to read it anyway.

I remember someone saying once—I expect it was a preacher on a stewardship Sunday—that people could tell where their treasure was buried by looking at their check stubs. I also remember a time-management consultant who said that one could tell what one's priorities were by looking at old calendars and appointment books. Which is, of course, why I seldom look at either.

"The difficulty with really seeing and really hearing is that we then really ought to do something about what we have seen and heard," said Buechner once. Which suggests that the way to avoid doing anything that really ought to be done is to avoid taking notice of it. Which is easier to do if you cannot actually remember the things that have happened to you.

From time to time, I will come to a stretch of days when I find myself avoiding my journal like the plague. I generally write in it at about the same time every day, and I have become pretty good at being able to fill up the time with other things when I need to. It is as though I think that if I can avoid those pages, I can avoid who I am being just now, I can avoid being held up to the light.

It is very hard to come face-to-face with God without coming face-to-face with myself, and vice versa. My life is where I am most likely to find Him, and when I run from my life, I run from the very thing

I seek, and from all the attendant possibilities for grace and clarity and reconciliation that God has in store.

A New York theater critic once said of a playwright that he lived "like any artist, perched somewhere between the marketplace and the marvelous," which is where my journal lives too. Or perhaps, between the marvelous and the mundane is more like it.

A journal goes with me pretty much everywhere I go. For one thing, I want to be ready just in case the marvelous strikes. It has not happened lately, but I have a pen and some blank pages with me at all times, just in case.

For another, I think a big black artist's sketchbook makes me look more literary when people run into me on the street. Fountain pens and vests and hats help too. Once I am famous and people are fighting over the right to publish my journals, there may be less need for such overt signals, but for now it helps. Right now, what usually happens after people ask me what I do and I tell them, they look at my sketchbook and my clothes and my fountain pen and say, "I knew you were a . . . *something*. . . ." Which may not be proof that I am actually anything after all, but at least I have the look down.

Because my journal is with me all the time, it ends up with all manner of things in it. Notes from telephone calls, postcards I receive and want to keep, church bulletins, quotations from books I am reading, sketches of gardening plans—all manner of stuff is just sort of piled in there alongside the stuff that I write when I sit down to journal. If I become as famous as you hope I do, then someone will publish *The Collected To-Do Lists of Robert Benson,* if for no other reason than that they are all there—I own no scratch pads.

The journals are one part history, one part prayer, one part confessional, one part meditation, one part storage facility, one part discipline, one part hope.

More than that, this is the one place where my own life intersects with the ancient traditions of the daily examen and confession. Where the thanksgivings are expressed in some deep way and where I discover blessings that have been hidden to me for years. It is the place where reconciliation begins, and accountability too, where promises made and promises broken are somehow mingled together to produce life.

On the whole, I wish it were more literary and less mundane. I wish it were more holy and less profane as well. I have reconciled myself to the fact that it will be of little value to anyone else, but I also know that it is far too precious for me to give it up.

There are some pages that have the feeling of prayer to them, some that even go so far as to begin, "Dear God," as though the salutation were necessary. There are some pages where it is so obvious that I was trying so hard to be so pious and so wise and so insightful that it is embarrassing. There are some pages where, by looking at the dates of the entries, it is clear that long periods went by without any prayer being offered at this particular altar.

When I come across the blank spaces, I suddenly feel lost, as though some portion of my life had gotten away and I have no memory of it. "I am now a kind of archive of people, places, and things that no longer exist," wrote the poet Philip Levine. "I carry them around with me, and if I get them on paper I give them at least some existence." Writing something down does not mean that it is not gone, but at least some portion of it remains for me to revisit and to remember, to recollect, as the saints would say.

From time to time, I find a page that has a

sentence that is at least honest and true, even though the truth of it may not have been apparent to me when I wrote it. It has become richer as it aged, hidden in a sketchbook, waiting for the book to be opened and the daylight to shine upon it again. One day I discovered the pages where I described my anger over the way I had been treated by my father once, and suddenly I saw that I had been nursing that anger for a long time and had not realized it. All the therapy in the world would never have brought it home to me in so real a way as did the few sentences scribbled in that old journal. Those few sentences, poorly but honestly written, about circumstances long forgotten held a key for me that had I known I had it, might well have unlocked a door or two sooner—doors that might well have changed everything in my life and in the lives of people I loved and now have lost. The process itself had worked better than I realized then, it just was not apparent to me at the time. But it is enough to remind me that it is right and good, for me at least, to keep scribbling every day.

There are some stretches in the journals that are so filled with loneliness and despair that it makes me ache just to remember the times when I wrote them. If I had realized how unhappy I was, I would have been more desperate than I was. But there are also stretches full of hope and joy and grace that came to me, and they make me sing and laugh and dance just to think of them.

I am glad that all of them are there. They would have been lost to me otherwise. And with them I would have lost the way in which the threads of my story are interwoven into the one Story that matters most, the Story that is the story of us all. The story that is held in the pile of sketchbooks on the top shelf in my studio is not only for me to tell, but for me to read. It is the only place where this story can be found. Without these journals—holy and profane, marvelous and mundane, precious and pretentious— there is no way ever to read or hold dear or discover the meaning of my story.

"Enlighten our hearts," we pray with the prayer book, "that we may remember in truth. . . ." Do not let us forget where we have been and where we had hoped to be, where we have come from and where we are going.

We take the pen and the page in our hands. What did happen this day or that one? In the time that elapsed after God said, "Let there be light," what did we do in the light we were given? Whom did we see and whom did we talk to, whom did we write and whom did we hear from, what did we read and what did we watch?

We note the weather and the news from home, or the conversation we had that signifies some new place in our lives. We take stock of our anxiety and our joy, we wonder "aloud" how the two can live side by side. There is a scribble and a doodle and a quote that we heard. There is a phrase caught in passing whose meaning is not yet clear. "It is as though each day is a treasure hunt," said Buechner, "and a journal is one way of seeing if you found the treasure that God has hidden for you this day."

"Examine your lives and conduct by the rule of God's commandments. . . ." Confession written can be as good as confession spoken. Forgiveness noted on paper can be a reminder of mercies to come.

There is the caller with whom you lost your temper, and the one who needs your help, the one you put off until another day. There is the one thing you promised to do that you ignored yet again, and the choice you made that was clearly the wrong one.

But there is also the remembrance of a moment of grace, and the smile of one you seem to have touched somehow. There is the gift you offered and the one you received, there is the wisdom you showed and the comfort you gave.

The collection of pages will show you a pattern and give you clues as to what must be done and what must be let go of. It will teach you how far you have come and how far you must go, and the source of your strength for the travels ahead.

"Grant that we may put our whole trust and confidence in Your mercy. . . ." Your own story begins to take shape in these pages, the tale of your own life along the Road Home. The threads of it, and its colors and textures, begin to reveal the ways of God in the Way that you travel.

You begin to get a glimpse here and there of who you really are. You begin to see who God has been to you. Your confidence and trust in God's mercy and providence begin to grow as you see how He has been with you.

"Direct us, O Lord, in all that we do . . . and further us with Your continual help," we pray, and begin to believe that He will, for we have seen such a thing in the story we have begun to tell ourselves on these pages.

. . .

My mother's father was the organist and choirmaster in a little Lutheran church for almost forty years. He had studied piano when he was young and hoped to be a classical performer, but that was not the way he spent his life.

He spent most all of his life living through one hard time or another. Some of his troubles came about by tragic circumstances that just sort of rolled over him and from which, in many ways, he never recovered. Some of his troubles were self-inflicted because of things about himself that he could not control or even understand.

In the midst of all these troubles, Sunday after Sunday, feast day after feast day, through illness and grief and pain, he got up, got himself to the little stone church with the red door and the stained-glass windows and the dwindling congregation to play for the service. I expect some days he played well and others pretty poorly. Life is like that for all of us, no matter what work we do.

The family all showed up to surprise him on the last Sunday he played before he retired. To save steps, he had long since stopped going the long way around to get to his place in the balcony at the back of the church before the services began, and he had come through the sanctuary, as was his custom now. He was surprised and pleased to see the dozen or so of us sitting there. He stopped and he bowed and he grinned ear to ear.

I went home and wrote in my journal about how rare it was to celebrate the fact that anyone has done anything for forty years. Staying with something for that long—work, marriage, ministry, friendship— through good and bad, joy and sorrow is not something we do much of these days.

I also realized that day that I had been scribbling in these journals for a long time. Not quite for forty years, but closer than I care to admit.

Some days for good, some days for something not so good, but at least scribbling nonetheless. And in that moment I began to sense what it means to discover the prayer of the heart, to get a whisper of the prayer of God that rises in my heart.

This pile of old sketchbooks is at least a sign of faithfulness of some sort. Faithfulness to the idea that it is important to keep a record of one's days in the belief that in their examination one can see the holy moments that have been granted. The sketchbooks signify a faithfulness to the proposition that the attempt to address the blank page armed with nothing more than a pen can be at least one act of courage and honesty in a day that may well yield more fear and insincerity than I would like to admit. Faithfulness to the hope that somewhere in the scribbling some measure of grace will begin to appear, even if it is only between the lines.

In the end, how well I make these prayers—the ones I make on these blank pages—is less important than the fact that I make them. What matters is that I come and sit here, that I hold my pen in my hand, that I balance my book in my lap, and that I wait to hear what comes to and from these pages. What matters is that I listen to my life. Anything profound or insightful is God's gift to me; it is the process, the oblation, that is my gift to God, paltry as it may be at times.

This way of prayer has been given to me, and to others, because it fits our hearts and our makeup. The feel of the paper, the scratching of the pen, the flickering of a candle, the early-morning darkness giving way to light, the quiet of the house.

If God speaks to me, it is here that it is most likely I will recognize His voice. There will be some days when I know it as I write it down, and many more when the truth of it can only be seen cumulatively. Looking back over such a record kept faithfully will reveal clues as to how my life and mind and heart and being have been shaped and transformed into what I am now, for better or for something far less than better. Such a record reveals a story that I can read and understand and value. Such a record offers the chance that I may meet God—while I am dancing on the head of a pen.

Something to Nail To

We know that all things are ordered by Your wisdom and love:
Grant us in all things to see Your hand;
that we may walk with Christ in all simplicity,
and serve You with a quiet and contented mind.

—From THE PROPER
FOR NOVEMBER 12

Sanctification is the entire process of obtaining holiness . . .
There is hardly any proper use of material things
which cannot thus be directed toward the sanctification of men
and the praise of God.

—On SANCTIFICATION

We fool ourselves if we think that such a sacramental way of living is
automatic. This kind of living communion does not just fall on our
heads. We must desire it and seek it out. . . . We must order our lives
in particular ways.

—RICHARD FOSTER

MY FATHER WAS THE ONE WHO taught me how to cut a board and drive a nail. I have even done both of those things straight a time or two, though not as often as I would have liked.

He would have taught me better, but by his own admission he was just a rough carpenter, not a "finish guy." When he was young, he pastored a small church in Florida, one of a series of such churches that he pastored. The church paid him a little bit and to help make ends meet, a man in the church had given him a job on a construction crew. It did not pay much either, but along with the school bus driving and the PE teaching at a nearby school, and the fact that we lived in four rooms at the back of the church, we did okay, I suppose. How would I know? I was six years old.

My father started out his construction crew career carrying boards and blocks and mixing concrete. Then he graduated to the framing crew. He had hopes of becoming a finish guy, but it turned out that he could not cut a straight board with a miter box, so he ended up working only on stuff that was going to get covered up by the real carpenters. Evidently he had trouble with driving nails straight too, because he told me once that he had seen boards die of lead poisoning on him before he could pound them into place. To my chagrin, I have discovered that the proclivity for killing boards in this manner is genetic.

But he loved to build things. And I grew up loving to help him. When we moved to Tennessee, to the big house that we all think of as the old home place, he helped to clear the land before the house could be built. He designed the house himself, and once it was up and we had moved in, he started in to work on it. He converted the garage into a family room, put an oak porch just outside the new room, poured a pebbled patio down by the lake, put in a rock retaining wall along the shoreline, ran a split-rail fence down the edge of the property, put in a brick sidewalk in the front and a brick patio in the back, hung a balcony on the back of the house, put up two basketball goals and a tree house, and dug two gardens and planted countless shrubs and trees across the four acres that ran down the hill to the lake.

I was right beside him most all the way. Some of my favorite memories are of working next to him on some project—cutting, hammering, building, digging, sweating, laughing, muttering under our breath at uncooperative nails. One of my most prized possessions is a piece of two-by-six where he and I tried to sketch out the risers for a set of stairs we built to go up to the loft studio that he helped me build in a house I once lived in. If he did not have a project to hammer on at his house, he would come and swing a hammer at yours if he found out that something was going up or coming down. We never did get the geometry for the risers just right. I heard later that the first thing the new owner did was to tear the steps out and have them replaced. She wanted some steps that did not have the character already built in, which is the way most of my carpentering comes out.

My father taught me to love old boards, the ones you reclaim from someone's old house or barn and haul home and cut and hammer into some new thing. One of the advantages is that they are already beat-up, so that if you miss a nail and hit a board a time or two or twenty-six, nobody notices. There is no real challenge to using new boards anyway. Anybody ought to be able to drive a straight nail into a piece of fresh pine. But if you can do that to a piece of oak that has been outside for twelve or fifteen years, then you have really done something. And if you cannot, you at least have an excuse. And a little built-in character to boot.

When the two years of the Academy were almost finished, I found that my original question—What might happen to me if I learned how to pray?—had begun to change. It began to sound more like this: *How* can a man like me, living a typical, harried, busy life in late-twentieth-century Western society, learn to pray?

There was no doubt that I knew more about prayer than I did before the Academy. And it was clear to me that some of what I had seen and learned and experienced at Sumatanga was drawing me toward a way to live that was different somehow. I found myself wanting to live a life that was centered in prayer rather than a life to which prayer was merely attached. How? was the question.

As terrifying as it seemed then, and as funny as it seems now, for a while I thought about entering a monastery. So many of the saints and pilgrims whose wisdom about the life of prayer has affected me so deeply happen to have lived in monastic settings. All I had to do was look at how much I loved the life at Sumatanga, with its quiet and order and separation from the noise and clamor of society, to begin to say to myself that such a life was the kind of life to which I was being drawn, at least by personality, and was perhaps even being called to by God.

But I was not then, and am not now, called to be a monk. I knew that, even as I recognized in myself the deep longing for a way to live a life of prayer in the midst of the place and work to which I am called, and with and for the people to whom I have been given.

Can such a life be lived only by those who live behind the walls of a monastery? Is such a life meant to be lived only by a chosen few? Is it only the monks who are called to pray without ceasing?

It seems to me sometimes that we who live as Christians in the twentieth-century world often live two lives. One is for Sundays and maybe Wednesdays. It is the life that we live for the church folks. The other life is the one that we live for the world of work and family and leisure. Serving two masters is probably no easier in our day than it was in the days when Jesus suggested that it was impossible. It may be even harder.

Nothing in our culture—not media, not politics, not business, not education, and sometimes not even our churches—is encouraging us to live lives that marry our religion with the rest of us. The culture we live in teaches us to get what we can, outsmart the other guy, vote for the folks who will protect our interests, buy everything that is not nailed down, and rent a storage facility if you cannot hold it all in the house you can barely afford. The Teacher calls us to give ourselves away, to stop worrying about tomorrow, to do good to the ones that hate us, to seek only the kingdom.

In the Buddhist tradition, the masters speak of practice, the cultivation of the mind and the heart. How do you practice what you believe to be true? they ask. When and how do you pray? How does what you believe in your heart become evident by the work that you do with your hands? How is it lived out in the way you spend your resources and time and money and energy? What are the tools that you use to explore and to cultivate the soil of your own life?

Saint Benedict might say it another way: What is your Rule?

Saint Benedict's Rule covers all manner of things that have to do with governing the life of a monastic community: when to eat, when to pray, how to take in newcomers, what to wear, how much mail one can send or receive, who is in charge when the abbot is away, and so on. When you read the Rule, it is clear that much of it has little to do with the day-to-day governance of a life lived in the way we live outside a monastic community.

If there was a point in time when we might have chosen Benedict's Rule to organize our society, we have missed it. For better or for worse, we have chosen differently. We live in neighborhoods where we do not know our neighbors, we make hour-long commutes to work, we watch television in the evenings rather than make conversation with our families and friends. We begin our day with the current incarnation of Bryant Gumbel rather than with the psalmist, we end our days with the late local news and weather and sports rather than confession and forgiveness and reconciliation.

At the heart of the Rule of Saint Benedict is the notion that above all a monastic community is "a school of prayer," a place where one might learn to live a life that is balanced between work, prayer, rest, and community, a life lived in such a way that it draws one closer and closer to a life lived in union with the One Who draws all men and women unto Himself. And somewhere deep in our hearts, perhaps whispered into us when the image of the Dreamer was breathed into us when we were whispered into being in the depths of the earth, is the longing for a way to live in which our work and our rest and our prayer and our community are not at odds with each other. We seek, one might say, a way to live one life instead of two.

One of the things that I carried away from my brief visits to Gethsemani was a growing suspicion that what I needed was not a new life but a new Rule by which to live the life I already have. I had a growing sense that I needed Saint Benedict's principles though not his Rule. I needed the frame but not the uniform.

Father Farrell often reminds me that "the three greatest obstacles to spiritual growth are amnesia, inertia, and mañana."

If I am to live the life that I seek, a life lived at attention, the life to which I believe I am called, then

I am going to have to do it on purpose. If I am to somehow balance a life between prayer and work and rest and community, then I am going to have to choose to do it, or at least to begin. It is not likely that it is just going to land on me. "We must exercise discipline in order to take control of our time," writes John McQuiston. "It is our ultimate currency."

To learn to pray the prayer to which I am called, I am going to have to pray. It will also be necessary for me to do some study and make some choices about the daily prayer that I will offer, about the places and the times, about the form and the method. I may well need a bell or a journal or a rug or a candle.

To do the work that I am given to do, I am going to need to do some homework. I am going to need to do some thinking and wondering and studying about my gifts and my talents. I am going to need to be sure that what I do with my hands actually comes from and nurtures my heart. I am going to have to examine its effects upon others and how it fits into the kingdom that has already come. And I am going to have to be clear about why I am doing it and my hopes and my dreams.

To have the rest—for my spirit and my mind and my body—that is needed to live a life that does not eat me alive, I am going to have to plan the ways in which I spend my days. I am going to have to make choices about time and attention, and about habits and diets and schedules and such. I am going to have to set aside days on my calendar to go away and be silent, and days to go and listen to those who can show me the Way. I am going to have to learn what Sabbath actually means and how to live it in my life.

To participate in the community of those to whom I have been given and who have been given to me, I am going to have to identify them, identify the ones that truly are the holy communities of which I am a part. I am going to need to be sure that my time and my resources are aimed in their direction, I am going to have to be clear about my role within them.

And if I think that all of this is going to happen without my making a list or two, I am kidding myself.

Years ago, in the days when I was masquerading as an actual contributing member of the business world, in my vice president's suit and my power necktie, there was a great movement that had to do with companies writing mission statements so that everyone would know what they were about. We used to spend an absolutely inordinate amount of time in management meetings arguing over what ours should say.

The meetings drove me crazy, generally speaking. I expect it was because I was not very good at things like consensus building and detaching myself from my ideas and such, the kinds of things that make for good executives and committee members and administrators. There is some connection between those things about me and the fact that I now work at home, by myself, and rarely go out into the world of work as it is practiced in our society.

I wish I had known about the Rule of Saint Benedict then. It is the best mission statement that I have ever seen. And it can be a guide for all of us who seek to develop a way of living our lives in the ways of prayer. It is not one that we can adopt in total, unless we are ready to move to the monastery, but it can be a starting point, a set of principles, a benchmark to use as we make our own rule of life.

It can be a place to begin to make those lists.

Notwithstanding all of the evidence to the contrary, I still think of myself as pretty handy with a hammer and such. I work in a studio that I built with my own two hands, and I put up a fence and a potting shed a couple of summers back, both of which are still standing. I even helped my brother and sister build a house to live in. I assumed I was pretty well near the top of the weekend carpenter heap until I saw George's cabin.

The first time I saw it I was already on the road to being intimidated. George was soon to be my brother-in-law, and the first Thanksgiving that my wife and I went there it was pretty much so that I could meet the family I was to become a part of.

George lives in a small town deep in the Mississippi Delta, about twenty miles from the Mississippi River. Actually George has a home and a business in the town, but where he really lives is at his cabin, which is only twenty yards from the river. Some years ago, he and some friends bought a long, thin stretch of wooded land between the levee and the water, and put up a gate and a sign that says: "Victoria Bend Hunt Club—Keep Out or Else." Then they put up cabins and such so that they could be there for weekends.

George bought an old shotgun house, the kind of long, one-story wooden house that is mostly used by tenant farmers throughout that part of the world. He had it hauled out to Victoria Bend and raised up onto telephone poles about twenty feet off the ground to keep it above the floodwaters that come through pretty regularly. Then he tore everything out of it and commenced to banging on it. When he started out, what he had up there in the air was an old run-down shack. When he finished, what he had was a two-bedroom cabin, with a gigantic screened porch, a huge deck, a kitchen big enough for fifteen people to eat in, and a grand view of one of the prettiest bends in the river.

George showed me around the place and I was suitably impressed. I did not stop to put a level on it anywhere, but it seemed like a pretty solid house to me. While we walked around we got to swapping war stories about building things armed with little more than a new hammer and a lot of nerve.

"I can build anything," he said, "as long as someone has put the first board in straight. I just need something to nail to."

A Rule—whether it is the Rule of Saint Benedict or the Rule of Gethsemani or even the Rule of Saint

Whatever-Your-Name-Is—holds no guarantee of anything much at all. But it can be a way to begin to show your gratitude and to come to attention. It can be a way for you to say with your time and your will that you will keep your promise to prepare a place should God choose to come and be with you. It is a way to remind yourself of the promises you made and the blessings you received in the mass, at the Eucharist, in the relationships to which you have been given.

Such a Rule is not the end of the journey of prayer, at best it is only the beginning. It is an altar of sorts, a place where you make your offerings and learn what must be sacrificed and begin to sense what might be gained should sacrifices be made.

But it is, at least, something to nail to.

"Oh, begin," said John Wesley. "Pray as if everything depended on God and work as if everything depended on you."

Write a Rule, make a list. Pay attention to the liturgy and the sacraments and the Word. Pray the office, keep a journal, take retreats. Find some time for some silence and some friends with whom to walk the

Road. Read some books, ask some questions, find some others who know.

Make a rule that is moderate, one you can keep. More will be added and taken away as you grow.

But begin, oh, begin. And take up your place in the general Dance.

Endnotes

THE EPIGRAPH PAGE PRECEDING EACH CHAPTER
has three elements.

The first epigraph on each page is an adaptation
of prayers from *The Book of Common Prayer,* the 1979
edition of the prayer book in use by the Episcopal
Church in America. It is published by the Church
Hymnal Corporation, New York.

The second epigraph has been taken from *The
Catholic Encyclopedia,* edited by Robert C. Broderick. It
is published by Thomas Nelson, Nashville.

The third epigraph is taken from one of the
writers of the books listed here. The list also includes
the names of other writers and books quoted
throughout the book. Some of the names will not be
found in the list. The questions are found in the
anthologies on the list or were part of private
discussions.

- Saint Benedict *The Rule of Saint Benedict*
  (The Liturgical Press: Collegeville, Minnesota)
- Bob Benson and Michael W. Benson *Disciplines for the Inner Life*
  (Thomas Nelson: Nashville)
- Dietrich Bonhoeffer *Letters and Papers from Prison*
  (SCM Press: New York)
- Frederick Buechner *The Sacred Journey; Now and Then; Telling Secrets; Listening to Your Life*
  (HarperCollins: San Francisco)
- Julia Cameron *The Vein of Gold*
  (Jeremy Tarcher: New York)
- Joseph Campbell *A Joseph Campbell Companion*
  (HarperCollins: San Francisco)
- Annie Dillard *The Writing Life; An American Childhood; Teaching a Stone to Talk*
  (HarperCollins: New York)
- Fr. Edward J. Farrell *Free to Be Nothing*
  (The Liturgical Press: Collegeville, Minnesota)
- Richard J. Foster *Freedom of Simplicity*
  (HarperCollins: New York)
- Peter France *Hermits*
  (St. Martin's Press: New York)
- Kahlil Gibran *The Prophet; Jesus the Son of Man*
  (Alfred A. Knopf: New York)

- Thich Nhat Hanh   *Living Buddha, Living Christ*
  (Riverhead Books: New York)
- John Ii McQuiston   *Always We Begin Again: The
  Benedictine Way of Living*
  (Morehouse Publishing: Harrisburg, Pennsylvania)
- Thomas Merton   *New Seeds of Contemplation*
  (Norton: New York); *The Courage for Truth; Thoughts
  in Solitude* (Farrar, Straus & Giroux: New York); *The
  Seven Storey Mountain* (Harcourt Brace: New York);
  The Journals of Thomas Merton, Volumes 1–7
  (HarperCollins: SanFrancisco)
- Claude Monet   *Monet by Himself*
  (Little, Brown: New York)
- M. Robert Mulholland   *Shaped by the Word*
  (Upper Room Books: Nashville)
- Kathleen Norris   *The Cloister Walk*
  (Riverhead Books: New York)
- Rodney Phillips, et al.   *The Hand of the Poet*
  (Rizzoli Books: New York)
- Rainer Maria Rilke   *Rilke's Book of Hours*
  (Riverhead Books: New York); *Letters to a Young Poet*
  (HarperCollins: San Francisco)
- Norman Shawchuck and Reuben P. Job   *A Guide to
  Prayer for Ministers and Other Servants*
  (Upper Room Books: Nashville)

- Huston Smith *The World's Religions*
  (HarperCollins: New York)
- Teresa of Avila *The Life of Saint Teresa of Avila by Herself*
  (Penguin Classics: New York)
- Studs Terkel *Working*
  (Pantheon Books: New York)
- Henry David Thoreau *On Walden Pond*
  (Random House: New York)
- Wendy Wright *The Vigil*
  (Upper Room Books: Nashville)

For information regarding THE ACADEMY FOR SPIRITUAL FORMATION: Danny Morris, The Upper Room, 1908 Grand Avenue, Nashville, Tennessee 37202 (615-340-7200).

About the Author

ROBERT BENSON writes, reads, keeps house, and says his prayers at his home in Hermitage, Tennessee. He can be persuaded to leave home to lead retreats on prayer and vocation, speak at conferences, go to baseball games and bookstores, and eat Italian food. He is happy to hear from fellow poets and pilgrims and always writes back when you write to him at the address below.

For information regarding retreats, writers' conferences, the Friends of Silence & of the Poor, or anything else that seems to be relevant to the mystery of prayer—or to be placed on the mailing list to receive a newsletter about such things—write to Robert Benson, Post Office Box 8177, Hermitage, Tennessee 37076.

A study guide for book groups and such is available from the above address.